A Nation of Takers

A NATION OF TAKERS

America's Entitlement Epidemic

Nicholas Eberstadt

Templeton Press
300 Conshohocken State Road, Suite 500
West Conshohocken, Pennsylvania, 19428
www.templetonpress.org

Designed and typeset by Gopa & Ted2, Inc.

Visit www.templetonpress.org to access complete sources for figures.

ISBN-13 978-1-59947-435-9

Library of Congress Cataloging-in-Publication Data on file

Printed in the United States of America

12 13 14 15 16 17   10 9 8 7 6 5 4 3 2 1

In memory of Daniel Patrick Moynihan
(1927–2003)

≥≤

Contents

≳≲

Acknowledgments   ix

PART I: *America's Growing Dependency
on Government Entitlements*

The Rise of Entitlements in Modern America, 1960–2010
Nicholas Eberstadt   3

PART II: *Dissenting Points of View*

Have We Become a "Nation of Takers"?
William A. Galston   93

Civil Society and the Entitlement State
Yuval Levin   115

Epilogue:
Response to Galston and Levin   129

About the Contributors   133

Acknowledgments

—— ⋛⋚ ——

THIS BOOK would not have come into being but for Susan Arellano of Templeton Press, whose idea it was that I write about the American entitlements question, and whose constant encouragement and sound guidance have made it much better than it would otherwise be. Ms. Kelly Matush provided exemplary research assistance over the course of this effort, as well as a keen eye to occasional lapses in my draft text. Ms. Jiyeon Song cheerfully offered expert help with some of the calculations and figures in this study, as well. Needless to say, I alone am responsible for any remaining errors. Gary Rosen of the *Weekend Review* for the *Wall Street Journal* did what every writer dreams his editor will do: He made my text sharper, more compelling, and more elegant in the excerpt he debuted in his pages. A special salute is due Sara Murray of the *Wall Street Journal*, who generously shared results from a Census Bureau analysis of entitlement program participation trends that had been commissioned by her paper. Conversations with Christopher C. DeMuth, long my boss at the American Enterprise Institute (AEI) and now Senior Fellow at the Hudson Institute, helped clarify my thoughts on several key questions. And it is Arthur C. Brooks, AEI's current president, who so far as I can tell first coined the phrase "nation of takers"—in any case, he first introduced me to it. I hope he won't mind the way it is used in the pages that follow.

Part I

≥≤

*America's Growing Dependency
on Government Entitlements*

The issue of welfare is the issue of dependency. It is different from poverty. To be poor is an objective condition; to be dependent, a subjective one as well. That the two circumstances interact is evident enough, and it is no secret that they are frequently combined. Yet a distinction must be made. Being poor is often combined with considerable personal qualities; being dependent rarely so. That is not to say that dependent people are not brave, resourceful, admirable but simply that their situation is never enviable, and rarely admired. It is an incomplete state of life: normal in a child, abnormal in an adult. In a world where completed men and women stand on their own feet, persons who are dependent—as the buried imagery of the word denotes—hang.

—*Daniel Patrick Moynihan, 1973*[1]

≥≤

The Rise of Entitlements in Modern America, 1960–2010

—— ≥≤ ——

INTRODUCTION

THE AMERICAN REPUBLIC has endured for more than two and a quarter centuries; the United States is the world's oldest constitutional democracy. But over the past fifty years, the apparatus of American governance has undergone a fundamental and radical transformation. In some basic respects—its scale, its preoccupations, even many of its purposes—the United States government today would be scarcely recognizable to a Franklin D. Roosevelt, much less an Abraham Lincoln or a Thomas Jefferson.

What is monumentally new about the American state today is the vast and colossal empire of entitlement payments that it protects, manages, and finances. Within living memory, the government of the United States of America has become an entitlements machine. As a day-to-day operation, the U.S. government devotes more attention and resources to the public transfers of money, goods, and services to individual citizens than to any other objective; and for the federal government, more to these ends than to all other purposes combined.

Government entitlement payments are benefits to which a person holds an established right under law (i.e., to which a person is entitled). A defining feature of these payments (also sometimes officially referred to as "current transfer receipts of individuals from government," or simply "transfers") is that they "are benefits received for which no current service is performed."[2] Entitlements are a relatively new concept in U.S. politics and policy; according to *Merriam-Webster*, the first known use of the term was not until 1942.[3] But entitlements have become very familiar, very fast. By the reckoning of the Bureau of Economic Analysis (BEA), the research group within the Commerce Department that prepares the U.S. government's GNP estimates and related national accounts, income from entitlement programs in the year 2010 was transferred to Americans under a panoply of over fifty separate types of programs, and accounted for almost one-fifth (18 percent) of personal income in that year.[4]

The breathtaking growth of entitlement payments over the past half-century is shown in Figure 1. In 1960, U.S government transfers to individuals from all programs totaled about $24 billion. By 2010, the outlay for entitlements was almost 100 times more. Over that interim, the nominal growth in entitlement payments to Americans by their government was rising by an explosive average of 9.5 percent per annum for fifty straight years. The tempo of growth, of course, is exaggerated by concurrent inflation—but after adjusting for inflation, entitlement payments soared more than twelve-fold

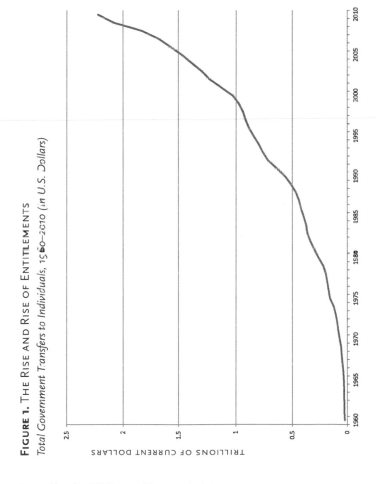

FIGURE 1. THE RISE AND RISE OF ENTITLEMENTS

Total Government Transfers to Individuals, 1960–2010 (in U.S. Dollars)

Source: Transfers: U.S. Bureau of Economic Analysis.

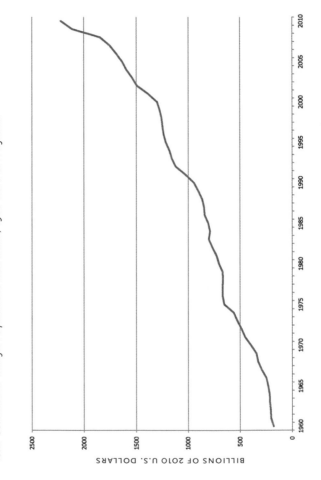

FIGURE 2. STILL EXPONENTIAL AFTER ALL THESE YEARS
Total Government Transfer Payments to Individuals, 1960–2010 CPI Adjusted

Sources: Transfers: U.S. Bureau of Economic Analysis.

CPI: U.S. Department of Labor, Bureau of Labor Statistics, consumer price index.

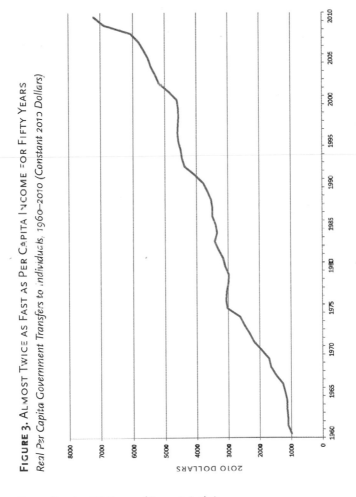

FIGURE 3. Almost Twice as Fast as Per Capita Income for Fifty Years
Real Per Capita Government Transfers to individuals, 1960–2010 (Constant 2010 Dollars)

Sources: Transfers: U.S. Bureau of Economic Analysis.
CPI: U.S. Department of Labor, Bureau of Labor Statistics, consumer price index.
Population: U.S. Census International Data Base.

(1248 percent), with an implied average real annual growth rate of about 5.2 percent per annum (see Figure 2).[5] Even after adjusting for inflation and population growth, entitlement transfers to individuals have more than septupled (727 percent) over the past half-century, rising at an overall average of about 4 percent per annum (see Figure 3).[6]

These long-term spending trends mask shorter-run tendencies, to be sure. Over the past two decades, for example, the nominal growth in these entitlement outlays has slowed to an average of "only" 7.1 percent a year (or a doubling every decade). Adjusted for inflation by the Consumer Price Index, real entitlement outlays rose by an average of "just" 4.4 percent over those years—and by a "mere" 3.2 percent a year on a per capita basis. But if the pace of entitlement growth has slowed in recent decades, so has the growth in per capita income. From 1960 to 2010 real per capita income in America grew by a measured 2.2 percent on average—but over the past twenty years, it has increased by 1.6 percent per annum.[7] In other words, total entitlement payouts on a real per capita basis have been growing twice as fast as per capita income over the past twenty years; the disparity between entitlement growth on the one hand and overall income growth on the other is greater in recent times than it was in earlier decades.

The magnitude of entitlement outlays today is staggering. In 2010 alone, government at all levels oversaw a transfer of over $2.2 trillion in money, goods, and services to recipient men, women, and children in the United States. At prevailing official exchange rates, that would have been greater than the entire GDP of Italy, roughly the equivalent of Britain's and close to the total for France—advanced economies all with populations of roughly 60 million each.[8] (The U.S. transfer numbers, incidentally, do not include the cost of administering the entitlement programs.) In 2010 the burden of entitlement transfers came to slightly more than $7,200 for every man, woman, and child in America. Scaled against a notional family of four, the average entitlements burden for that year alone would have approached $29,000. And that payout required payment from others, through taxes, borrowing, or some combination of the two.

A half-century of unfettered expansion of entitlement outlays has completely inverted the priorities, structure, and functions of federal administration, as these had been understood by all previous generations of American citizens. Until 1960 the accepted purpose of the federal government, in keeping with its constitutional charge, was governing. The federal government's spending patterns reflected that mandate. The overwhelming share of federal expenditures was allocated to defending the republic against enemies foreign and domestic (defense, justice, interest payments on the national debt) and some limited public services and infrastructural investments (the postal authority, agricultural extension, transport infrastructure, and the like). Historically, transfer payments did not figure prominently (or, sometimes, at all) in our federal ledgers. The Bureau of Economic Analysis (BEA), which prepares

America's GNP estimates and related national accounts, identifies only two calendar years before 1960 in which federal transfer payments exceeded other federal expenditures: in 1931, with President Herbert Hoover's heretofore unprecedented public relief programs, and in 1935, under President Roosevelt. (Even then, given the limited size of the U.S. government in those years, these entitlement transfers were negligible from a contemporary perspective—totaling just over 3 percent of GDP in 1931, and under 3 percent in 1935.[9]) For most of FDR's tenure, and for much of the Great Depression, the share of federal spending devoted to income transfers was a third or less of total spending.

In 1960, entitlement program transfer payments accounted for well under one-third of the federal government's total outlays (see Figure 4)—about the same fraction as in 1940, when the Great Depression was still shaping American life, with unemployment running in the range of 15 percent. But then—in just a decade and a half—the share of entitlements in total federal spending suddenly spurted up from 28 percent to 51 percent. It did not surpass the 50 percent mark again until the early 1990s. But over the past two decades it rose almost relentlessly, until by 2010 it accounted for just about two-thirds of all federal spending, with all other responsibilities of the federal government—defense, justice, and all the other charges specified in the Constitution or undertaken in the intervening decades—making up barely one-third (see Figures 5 and 6). Thus, in a very real sense, American governance has literally turned upside-down by entitlements—and within living memory.

The story of the (im)balance between entitlement transfers and overall government activities—at the federal, state, and local levels—is none too different (see Figures 7 and 8). In 1940, federal government transfers to individuals amounted to under one-sixth of total U.S. government outlays; in 1960, twenty years later, these entitlements still comprised barely 19 percent of all U.S. government expenditures. Between 1960 and 2010, the share of entitlements in government spending at all levels jumped from 19 percent to 43 percent—and the ratio of non-entitlement to entitlement spending fell from 4.2:1 down to 1.3:1. On that trajectory, the day in which entitlement spending comes to exceed all other activities of all levels and branches of the U.S. government is already within sight.

Although the U.S. entitlements archipelago is by now extraordinarily far-flung and complex, with dozens upon dozens of separate programmatic accounts extant today, the overall structure of government entitlement spending can be classified into just a few categories. U.S. public transfer data are easily divided into six overall baskets: income mainte-nance, Medicaid, Medicare, Social Security, unemployment insurance, and all the others (see Figures 9 and 10). Broadly speaking, the first two baskets attend to entitlements based upon poverty or income status; the second two, entitlements attendant upon aging or old-age status; and the next, entitle-

FIGURE 4. THE U.S. GOVERNMENT BECOMES AN ENTITLEMENT MACHINE
Federal Government Entitlement Transfers as a Percent of Federal Budget Outlays, 1940–2010

Sources: Federal Government Entitlement Transfers: Bureau of Economic Analysis.
Federal Budget Outlays: White House Fiscal Year 2012 Historical Tables, Table 1.1.

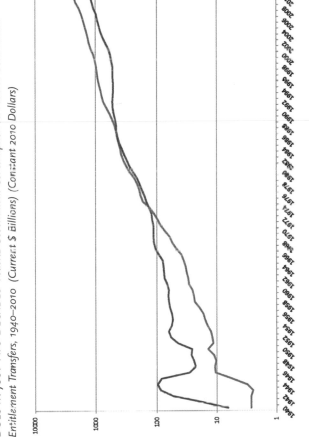

FIGURE 5. TRANSFERS DISPLACED EVERYTHING ELSE THE FEDERAL GOVERNMENT DOES IN JUST TWO DECADES *Federal Government Consumption vs. Federal Government Entitlement Transfers, 1940–2010 (Current $ Billions) (Constant 2010 Dollars)*

GOVERNMENT TRANSFERS   ──────   FEDERAL GOVERNMENT CONSUMPTION

Sources: Government Entitlement Transfers: Bureau of Economic Analysis.
Federal Government Consumption.

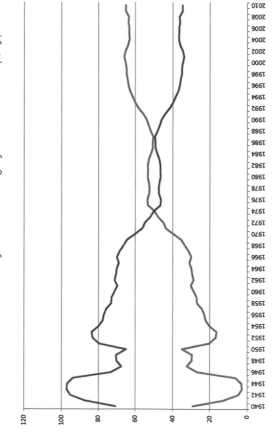

FIGURE 6. THE ENTITLED STATES OF AMERICA   *Federal Government Consumption vs. Federal Government Entitlement Transfers as a Percentage of Total Federal Outlays, 1940–2010*

— PERCENTAGE TRANSFERS OF TOTAL

— PERCENTAGE CONSUMPTION (FEDERAL) OF TOTAL

Sources: Government Entitlement Transfers: Bureau of Economic Analysis.
Federal Government Consumption.

FIGURE 7. In Transfers We Trust—Increasingly   *Total Government Consumption vs. Federal Government Entitlement Transfers (In Billions) (Constant 2010 Dollars)*

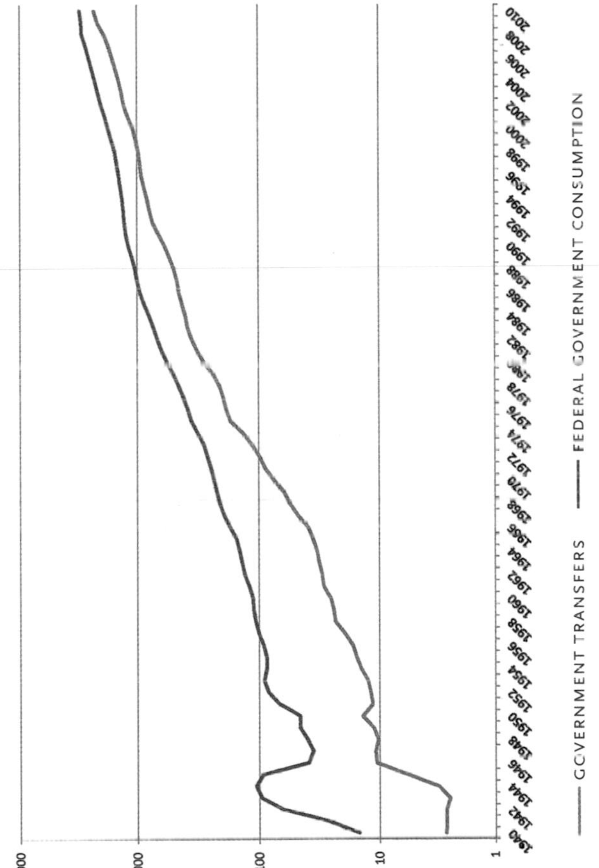

GOVERNMENT TRANSFERS   FEDERAL GOVERNMENT CONSUMPTION

Sources: Entitlement Transfers: Bureau of Economic Analysis.

Total Government Consumption.

FIGURE 8. PREPARE FOR CROSSOVER . . .

*Total Government Consumption vs. Federal Government Entitlement Transfers
as a Percent of Government Outlays at All Levels, 1940–2010*

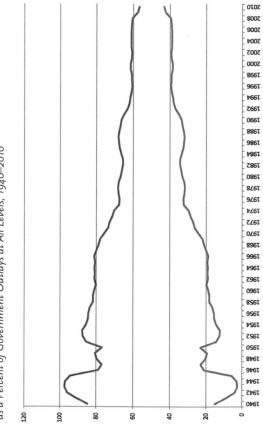

Sources: Government Entitlement Transfers: Bureau of Economic Analysis1.
Federal Government Consumption.

FIGURE 9. COMPOSITION OF TOTAL GOVERNMENT TRANSFER PAYMENTS, 1960–2010 (CURRENT DOLLARS)

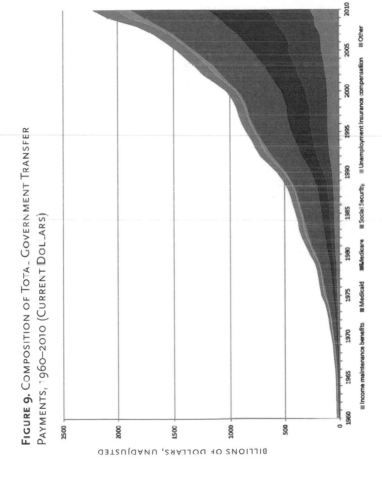

Source: Transfer payments: Bureau of Economic Analysis.

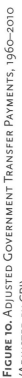

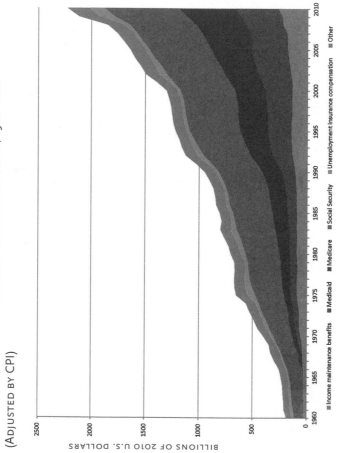

Figure 10. Adjusted Government Transfer Payments, 1960–2010 (Adjusted by CPI)

Sources: Transfer payments: Bureau of Economic Analysis1.

U.S. Department of Labor, Bureau of Labor Statistics, Consumer Price Index.

ments based upon employment status. The first five of these entitlement categories account for about 90 percent of total government transfers to individuals, and the first four categories comprise about five-sixths of all such spending. These four bear closest consideration.

Poverty- or income-related entitlements—transfers of money, goods, or services, including health-care services—accounted for over $650 billion in government outlays in 2010 (see Figure 11). Between 1960 and 2010, inflation-adjusted transfers for these objectives increased by over thirty-fold, or by over 7 percent a year; significantly, however, income and benefit transfers associated with traditional safety-net programs now comprise only about a third of entitlements granted on income status, while two-thirds of those allocations are absorbed by the health-care guarantees offered through the Medicaid program.

For their part, entitlements for older Americans worked out to even more: by 2010, about $1.2 trillion (see Figure 12).[10]

In real terms, these age-related transfers multiplied by a factor of about 12 over that period—or an average of more than 5 percent a year. But in purely arithmetic terms, the most astonishing growth of entitlements has been for health-care guarantees based on claims of age (Medicare) or income (Medicaid) (see Figure 13). Until the mid-1960s, no such entitlements existed; by 2010, these two programs were absorbing more than $900 billion annually.

In current political discourse, it is common to think of the

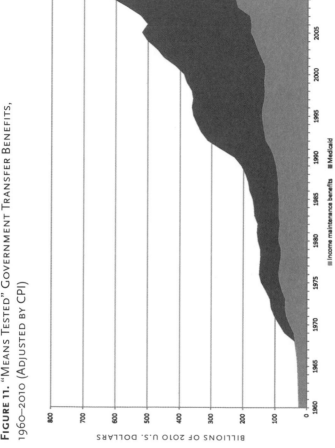

FIGURE 11. "MEANS TESTED" GOVERNMENT TRANSFER BENEFITS, 1960–2010 (ADJUSTED BY CPI)

Sources: Transfer payments: Bureau of Economic Analysis.

U.S. Department of Labor, Bureau of Labor Statistics, Consumer Price Index.

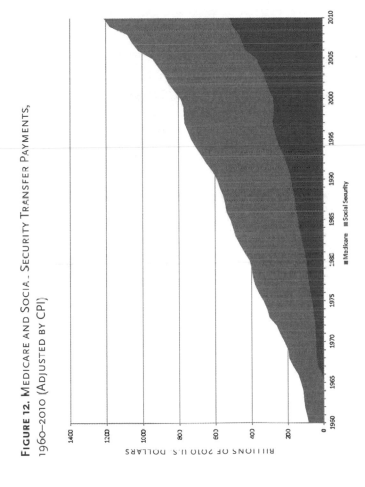

FIGURE 12. MEDICARE AND SOCIAL SECURITY TRANSFER PAYMENTS, 1960–2010 (ADJUSTED BY CPI)

Sources: Transfer payments. Bureau of Economic Analysis.
U.S. Department of Labor, Bureau of Labor Statistics, Consumer Price Index.

FIGURE 13. GOVERNMENT TRANSFER PAYMENTS, FOR MEDICARE AND MEDICAID, 1960–2010 (ADJUSTED BY CPI)

Sources: Transfer payments: Bureau of Economic Analysis.

U.S. Department of Labor, Bureau of Labor Statistics, Consumer Price Index.

Democrats as the party of entitlements—but long-term trends seem to tell a somewhat different tale. From a purely statistical standpoint, the growth of entitlement spending over the past half-century has in truth been distinctly greater under Republican administrations than Democratic ones. Between 1960 and 2010, to be sure, the growth of entitlement spending was exponential—but in any given calendar year, it was on the whole over 8 percent higher if the president happened to be a Republican rather than a Democrat.[11] This is in keeping with the basic facts of the time: notwithstanding the criticisms of "big government" that emanated from their Oval Offices from time to time. The Richard Nixon, Gerald Ford, and George W. Bush administrations presided over especially lavish expansions of the American entitlement state. Irrespective of the reputations and the rhetoric of the Democratic and Republican parties today, the empirical correspondence between Republican presidencies and turbocharged entitlement expenditures should underscore the unsettling truth that both political parties have, on the whole, been working together in an often unspoken consensus to fuel the explosion of entitlement spending in modern America.

THE NEW AMERICAN WAY OF LIFE: OUR NATIONAL DECLARATION OF DEPENDENCE

From the founding of our state up to the present—or rather, until quite recently—the United States and the citizens who peopled it were regarded, at home and abroad, as "exceptional" in a number of deep and important respects. One of these was their fierce and principled independence, which informed not only the design of the political experiment that is the U.S. Constitution but also the approach to everyday affairs. The proud self-reliance that struck Alexis de Tocqueville in his visit to the United States in the early 1830s extended to personal finances. The American "individualism" about which he wrote included social cooperation, and on a grand scale—the young nation was a hotbed of civic associations and voluntary organizations. Rather, it was that American men and women viewed themselves as accountable for their own situation through their own achievements in an environment bursting with opportunity—a novel outlook at that time, markedly different from the prevailing Old World (or at least Continental) attitudes.

The corollaries of this American ethos (which might be described as a sort of optimistic Puritanism) were, on the one hand, an affinity for personal enterprise and industry; and, on the other hand, a horror of dependency and contempt for anything that smacked of a mendicant mentality. Although many Americans in earlier times were poor—before the twentieth century, practically everyone was living on income that would be considered penurious nowadays[12]—even people in fairly desperate circumstances were known to refuse help or handouts as an affront to their dignity and independence. People who subsisted on public resources were known as "paupers," and provision for these paupers was a local undertaking. Neither beneficiaries nor recipients held the condition of pauperism in high regard.[13]

Overcoming America's historic cultural resistance to government entitlements has been a long and formidable endeavor. But as we know today, this resistance did not ultimately prove an insurmountable obstacle to the establishment of a mass public entitlements regime or to the normalization of the entitlement lifestyle in modern America. The United States is at the verge of a symbolic threshold: the point at which more than half of all American households receive, and accept, transfer benefits from the government. From cradle (strictly speaking, from *before* the cradle) to grave, a treasure chest of government-supplied benefits is open for the taking for every American citizen—and exercising one's legal rights to these many blandishments is now part and parcel of the American way of life.

Just how the great American postwar migration to general entitlement dependency was accomplished will be a matter for future historians to explain. For now we can note that there was a certain supply-and-demand dynamic was in play—and in this saga, supply helped to create its own demand. Government purveyed, and to sell these particular wares effectively, it was necessary for government to get into the business of norm-changing. A succession of presidential administrations did just that, with continuing dedication and some ingenuity. Two of the many milestones in this effort deserve brief mention here.

The first is the promulgation of the electronic benefit transfer (EBT) card, which began its march through the federal entitlement apparatus in the 1990s. EBTs were issued in the place of food stamps—coupons that could be used at grocery stores but which were made to look different from cash, and which carried restrictions on what the possessor could purchase. EBTs, in contrast, were plastic swipe cards basically indistinguishable from ordinary debit or credit cards. In 2008—under President George W. Bush—the Supplemental Farm Bill, which had always previously spoken of food "stamps" and "coupons," struck those words from the law and replaced all mention of these possibly stigmatizing instruments with "EBT" and "card."[14]

More recently, President Barack H. Obama offered an encomium to the new lifelong procession of entitlements—as advertisements for his 2012 reelection campaign. These feature an imaginary woman named "Julia," who is shown to benefit from government transfers and programs from preschool (Head Start) to childbearing (Medicaid, the Affordable Care Act) to working ages (loans from the Small Business Administration) to retirement (Social Security and Medicare).[15] In this important new political departure, entitlements and social welfare programs are no longer reluctantly defended, but instead positively celebrated as part of the American dream: and the promise to not only defend these but to increase their scope still further is offered as a positive reason for Obama's reelection.

Whatever the particulars of the supply-demand interaction, the plain fact is that the utilization of government entitlement benefits by American citizens registered what epidemiologists would call a "breakout" into the general population over the past two generations. Figures 14 and 15 detail one dimension of that breakout: the average share of personal income derived from government transfer benefits. (These were commissioned by the *New York Times* in conjunction with a major article on the prevalence of entitlement dependency in middle-class America[16] and afford even more detail in their interactive online version.[17]) According to this work, relying upon data from the Bureau of Economic Analysis (BEA) and the Census Bureau, the share of government transfer benefits in overall personal income for the nation as a whole rose from under 8 percent to almost 18 percent in the four decades between 1969 and 2009. (To be sure, 2009 was an unusually bad year for the American economy, but the long-term trend, decade by decade, was unmistakably upward: and the ratio continued upward in 2010, even though that was ostensibly a year of economic recovery.)

Given the obvious arithmetic fact that many of the United States' three-thousand-plus counties had to register above these national averages, the geography of entitlement dependency perforce suggested some remarkable extremes by 2010. By 2010, the populations of many U.S. counties were deriving more than 40 percent of personal income from government transfers to individuals and related entitlement benefits.

FIGURE 14. THE RISING TIDE OF ENTITLEMENTS, PART I

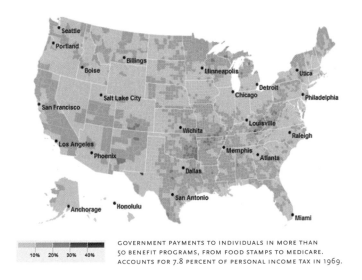

GOVERNMENT PAYMENTS TO INDIVIDUALS IN MORE THAN
50 BENEFIT PROGRAMS, FROM FOOD STAMPS TO MEDICARE.
ACCOUNTS FOR 7.8 PERCENT OF PERSONAL INCOME TAX IN 1969.

Source: *The New York Times*, "The Geography of Government Benefits,"
February 11, 2012.

But interestingly enough, in 2010 the most extreme county-level dependence on government transfers tended to be in rural areas rather than urban ones, and in red states rather than blue states. According to the estimates by the aforementioned *New York Times* team, in fact, two-thirds of the one hundred most dependent counties in America voted for the Republican rather than the Democratic candidate in the 2008 presidential election.[18] Thus we can see another particularity of daily life in many reaches of entitlement America:

FIGURE 15. THE RISING TIDE OF ENTITLEMENTS, PART II

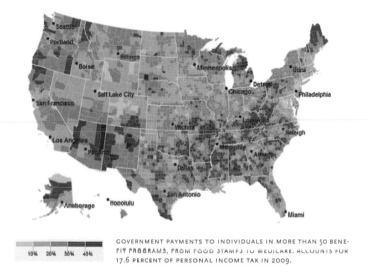

GOVERNMENT PAYMENTS TO INDIVIDUALS IN MORE THAN 50 BENE-
FIT PROGRAMS, FROM FOOD STAMPS TO MEDICARE. ACCOUNTS FOR
17.6 PERCENT OF PERSONAL INCOME TAX IN 2009.

Source: *The New York Times*, "The Geography of Government Benefits,"
February 11, 2012

to wit, the methodical arrangement of personal affairs to draw growing support from public transfers by many of the very people who are unselfconsciously professing to prefer a smaller American government.

Overall regional ratios of government transfers to personal income cannot speak to another dimension of the entitlement epidemic, which is the prevalence of government transfer recipience. Such estimates, however, can be derived from the Census Bureau's survey data and from administrative records of the entitlement programs themselves, although these two sources tend to give consistently different readings (albeit parallel ones over time). Like some other sources of income, including dividends and interest, government benefits tend to be seriously underreported by recipients in surveys. A 2004 study by the BEA and Census Bureau researchers, for example, estimated for the year 2001 that the Census Bureau's tallies undercounted means-tested income transfers by two-fifths, and disability benefits by two-thirds even after official Census adjustments for underreporting.[19] By the same token, a 2007 study by a researcher at the Urban Institute found for the year 2002 that the Census Bureau's Survey of Income and Program Participation (SIPP) figures understated the actual administrative caseload of the food stamp program by 17 percent, Medicaid/State Children's Health Insurance Program (SCHIP) by 20 percent, and Temporary Assistance for Needy Families (TANF) (the successor to Aid to Families with Dependent Children [AFDC]) by over 40 percent—and that the performance of the Census's Current Population Survey (CPS) was even worse.[20] All of which is to say that the true levels of entitlement recipience in America are even higher than the Census Bureau estimates indicate.

According to a Census Bureau data run requested by the *Wall Street Journal*, just over 49 percent of America's population lived in households that were using at least one government benefit to help support themselves in early 2011[21] (see Figure 16). This represented a tremendous increase over the early 1980s, at which time just under 30 percent of Americans were estimated to live in homes drawing entitlements from at least one of the government's many benefit programs. Over the past generation, in other words, the share of Americans accepting transfers from the U.S. government has jumped by very nearly 20 percentage points. That rise, however, was not entirely uninterrupted. In the late 1990s (in the aftermath of welfare reform and at a time of relatively robust economic growth), the prevalence of benefit recipience declined temporarily before continuing on its further ascent.

If the Census Bureau reports that over 49 percent of Americans are obtaining at least one government benefit, we can safely say that the true number is actually already well over 50 percent. To put it another way: a majority of American voters live in homes now applying for and obtaining one or more benefits from U.S. government programs.[22]

The prevalence of entitlement program usage is by no means uniform by age group or ethnicity. Meaningful variations within American society and the public at large are illustrated in Figures 17, 18, and 19. In 2004, according to a study based on Current Population Survey (CPS) microdata conducted by a researcher at American Association of Retired Persons (AARP), nearly 48 percent of American families were already obtaining at least one government benefit (a somewhat higher fraction than Census Bureau researchers indicated for 2004 in Figure 16, perhaps because recipient households tend to be slightly smaller than non-recipient

FIGURE 16. EXPANDING NET

Percentage of U.S. Population Living in a Household Receiving Some Government Benefit

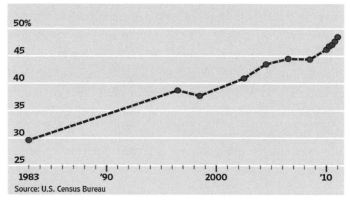

Source: U.S. Census Bureau

Source: Sara Murray, *Wall Street Journal*, "Nearly Half of U.S. Lives in Household Receiving Government Benefit," October 5, 2011.

households). By these numbers, nearly every household (98 percent) with someone sixty-five or older was obtaining at least one benefit, with 95 percent of them obtaining benefits from two programs. Generally speaking, these would be Medicare and Social Security/Old-Age and Survivors Insurance (OASI).[23]

Perhaps more striking, though, is the proportion of households with *no one* sixty-five or older obtaining government benefits: entitlement prevalence for this group was already at 35 percent in the year 2004. Relatively few of these beneficiaries were Social Security/OASI or Medicare cases—and of the

FIGURE 17.

RECEIPT OF MULTIPLE GOVERNMENT BENEFITS
AMONG FAMILIES IN 2004

Number of Government Benefits	Families with Person(s) Age 65 and Over		Families without Person Age 65 and Over		All Families	
	Number of Families N (in 1,000)	Percent of All Families (%)	Number of Families N (in 1,000)	Percent of All Families (%)	Number of Families N (in 1,000)	Percent of All Families (%)
At least one benefit	23,118	97.7	31,501	34.8	54,619	47.8
At least two benefits	22,530	95.2	15,899	17.6	38,429	33.7
At least three benefits	7,775	32.9	8,037	8.9	15,816	13.9
At least four benefits	1,887	5.4	3,538	1.4	4,922	4.3

Source: Ke Bin Wu, AARP Public Policy Institute, "Receipt of Entitlement and Other Safety-net Program Benefits among Families in 2011," April 2007. Original source: U.S. Census Bureau, March 2005.

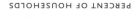

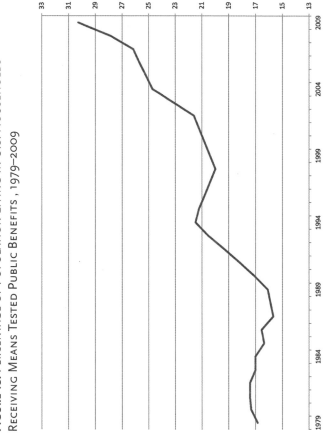

FIGURE 18. PERCENTAGE OF POPULATION LIVING IN U.S. HOUSEHOLDS RECEIVING MEANS TESTED PUBLIC BENEFITS, 1979–2009

Source: Sara Murray, *Wall Street Journal*, "Nearly Half of U.S. Lives in Household Receiving Government Benefit," October 5, 2011.

Household Percents: U.S. Census Bureau Statistical Abstracts, 1980–2012.

FIGURE 19. PERCENTAGE OF PERSONS LIVING IN HOUSEHOLDS RECEIVING SELECTED NONCASH BENEFITS: 2009, (BY AGE AND ETHNICITY)

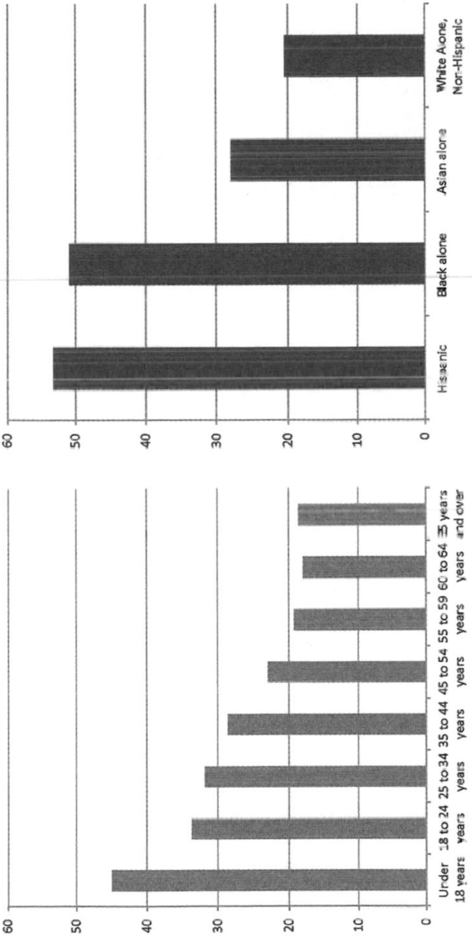

Source: 2012 Statistical Abstract, Table 543—Persons Living in Households Receiving Selected Non Cash Benefits: 2009.

rest, only a minority was accounted for by unemployment or disability benefits. The overwhelming majority instead were accounted for by households and families availing themselves of means-tested benefits or "antipoverty" programs: of the 35 percent on entitlements of any sort, nearly 23 percent were receiving "need-related" benefits.

As may be seen in Figure 18, the proportion of Americans accepting means-tested benefits has soared over the past three decades.[24] According to data from the Census SIPP survey, which began in the late 1970s, the share was just under 17 percent in 1979, but over 30 percent by 2009—and since recipience is understated in SIPP, the actual level is already higher than this. In any case, according to Census Bureau estimates, as of 2009 roughly 4 percent of Americans lived in public housing; 6 percent of Americans lived in households receiving some means-tested cash assistance, 11 percent in households accepting food stamps, and almost 25 percent in households accepting Medicaid.[25] Suffice it to say that the welfare reforms of the 1990s obviously have had no lasting impact on the long-term spread of "need related" entitlement dependency.

The habituation of Americans to life on entitlement benefits has already progressed much further than many of us might realize. As of 2009, an estimated 45 percent of all American children under eighteen years of age were receiving at least one form of means-tested government aid. It is quite possible, considering the scale of underreporting in these surveys, that a majority today are getting benefits from government antipoverty programs. An outright majority of Hispanic and African Americans of all ages were living in household reportedly using such programs, as well as almost 30 percent of Asian Americans and over 20 percent of non-Hispanic whites or "Anglos."

It is worth noting, incidentally, that the level of means-tested benefit dependency for Anglos today is almost as high as it was for black Americans when Daniel Patrick Moynihan was prompted to write his famous report on the crisis in the African American family,[26] (although the degree of dependency on government entitlements for the families in question is arguably not nearly as extreme today among the former as it was in the early 1960s among the latter). In another eerie echo of the Moynihan Report, we may see today exactly the same statistical "scissors" nationwide opening up between trend lines in unemployment rates and welfare benefits that moved Moynihan to alarm about conditions in the African American community nearly half a century ago (see Figure 20).

Over the three decades 1979–2009, the unemployment rate has risen, and fallen, and risen again in successive cycles—but the proportion of Americans living in households seeking and receiving means tested benefits has moved in an almost steady upward direction, essentially unaffected by the gravitational pull of the unemployment rate. The same is true for the relationship between means-tested benefits and the official poverty rate for American families (see Figure 21).

Even together, the unemployment rate and the family poverty rate provide almost no predictive information for tracking the trajectory of the proportion of American families obtaining one or more means-tested benefits. (By 2009 the share of American families receiving poverty-related entitlements was almost three times as high as the official poverty rate for families—and it was well over three times as high as the national unemployment rate.) There is one predictor of this "family dependency rate," however, that happens to be fearfully good—and this is calendar year. All other things being equal, the family dependency rate was on a relentless rise between 1979 and 2009; after controlling for the reported unemployment and family poverty rates, dependency was nevertheless increasing by over four percentage points every decade.[27] On this track, it will only be a matter of time before a majority of Americans are seeking and obtaining "anti-poverty" benefits from the government—regardless of their wealth or their employment prospects.

Entitlement recipience—even means-tested entitlement recipience—is now a Main Street phenomenon in modern America, a truly amazing turn of events for the nation of legatees to the Declaration of Independence. Entitlement dependence comes at great cost—and, as Moynihan warned nearly forty years ago, "It cannot too often be stated that the issue of welfare is not what it costs those who provide it, but what it costs those who receive it."[28] In the next pages we discuss some of these costs to its entitlements' recipients.

FIGURE 2C. DISCONNECT:

Households Receiving Means Tested Public Benefits (%) vs. Unemployment Rate, 1979–2009

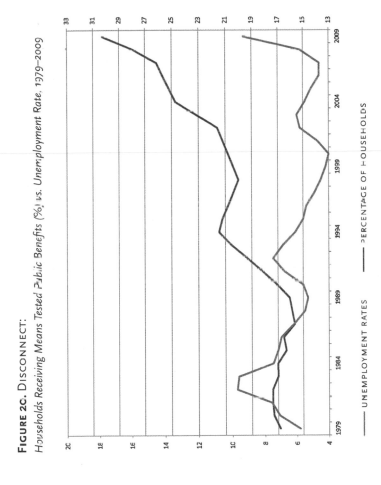

Source: Sara Murray, *Wall Street Journal*, "Nearly Half of U.S. Lives in Household Receiving Government Benefit," October 5, 2011.

Household Percents: U.S. Census Bureau Statistical Abstracts, 1980–2012.

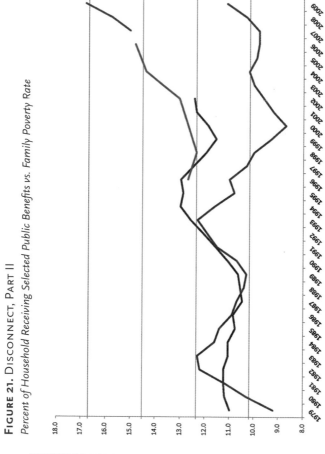

FIGURE 21. DISCONNECT, PART II

Percent of Household Receiving Selected Public Benefits vs. Family Poverty Rate

——— PERCENT OF HOUSEHOLDS RECEIVING MEANS-TESTED NONCASH
BENEFITS

——— PERCENT OF HOUSEHOLDS RECEIVING SELECTED SOURCES
OF NONCASH BENEFITS AND CASH TRANSFER PAYMENTS

——— PERCENT OF PERSONS LIVING IN HOUSEHOLDS RECEIVING
SELECTED NONCASH BENEFITS

——— FAMILY POVERTY LEVEL

THE MALE FLIGHT FROM WORK
IN THE ENTITLEMENT SOCIETY

The omnipresence of entitlements and their attendant panoply of temptations have already markedly altered what was formerly known as the American way of life, as well as the value structure that supported it. This result should hardly surprise anyone. With personal dependence on government handouts not only destigmatized, but increasingly enshrined as a basic civil right of all American citizens, mass behavior and popular attitudes could not help but mutate—often in highly uncivil directions.

The adverse influence of transfer payments on family values and family formation in America is one of these critical consequences. Important as it is, this is already old news. The deterioration of the postwar U.S. family structure under the shadow of a growing welfare state was a topic that had already attracted comment for decades before Charles Murray's seminal study, *Losing Ground*, [29] appeared almost thirty years ago. Murray's exegesis formally explained what many concerned citizens had already suspected or concluded: that

Sources (Fig. 21): Family Poverty Rate: U.S. Census Bureau Historical Poverty Tables—Families, Table 13. Number Below Poverty Level and Rate, http://www.census.gov/hhes/www/poverty/data/historical/families.html.

Household Percents: U.S. Census Bureau Statistical Abstract, 1980–2012, http://www.census.gov/compendia/statab/.

Sara Murray, *Wall Street Journal*, "Nearly Half of U.S. Lives in Household Receiving Government Benefit," October 5, 2011, http://blogs.wsj.com/economics/2011/10/05/nearly-half-of-households-receive-some-government-benefit/.

the perverse incentives embedded in federal-family support policies were actually encouraging the proliferation of fatherless families and an epidemic of illegitimacy. Although the Aid for Families with Dependent Children (AFDC) program had been established back in the 1930s to provide for orphans, by the early 1980s paternal orphans accounted for just 1 percent of the AFDC caseload; by 1982 nearly half of the children on AFDC qualified because their mothers were unwed, and three-fifths of the children of never-married mothers were receiving AFDC payments.[30] It may suffice to say that AFDC and its allied benefit programs had, by those specifications, incontestably become a vehicle for financing single motherhood and the out-of-wedlock lifestyle in America. The tangled pathology linking entitlement programs to the feminization of poverty and the rise of the female-headed family was addressed, after a fashion, by the welfare reform efforts of the mid-1990s (about which more later).

While the insidious effects of entitlement programs on the lifestyles of women and children have occasioned tremendous attention since the end of World War II, much less has been devoted to their consequences for men. American manhood, however, has not been left untouched by the entitlements revolution. Before the age of entitlements, self-reliance and the work ethic were integral and indispensable of the ideal of manliness in America. Able-bodied men who did not support themselves were shamed—and quite commonly, ashamed: the epithet "shiftless" was reserved for such men, and they were widely looked down upon by other Americans, irrespective of age, gender, or ethnicity.

The world is very different today. The dignity of work no longer has the same call on men as in earlier times. Over the past several generations, America has come to accept a huge move out of employment by men—in an era when work was readily available and when jobs were taken up increasingly by women. Put simply, the arrival of the entitlement society in America has coincided with a historically unprecedented exit from gainful work by adult men.

Figure 22 frames the dynamic by outlining trends in the labor force participation rate—the ratio of persons working or seeking work in relation to the total reference population. From 1948 to 2011 the overall labor force participation rate for American adults age twenty and over rose—from about 59 percent to about 66 percent, despite the 2008 crash. But this arithmetic average is the confluence—really, a convergence—of two very different trends. Since 1948 the U.S. female labor force participation rate has soared: from about 32 percent to almost 60 percent. But over those same years, the male labor force participation rate plummeted: from about 89 percent to just 73 percent. Labor force participation rates for men and women are closer today than ever before—not only because of the inflow of women into the workforce but also because of the withdrawal of men.

Under the force of these trends, men are literally becoming less important than women in keeping America at work. Over

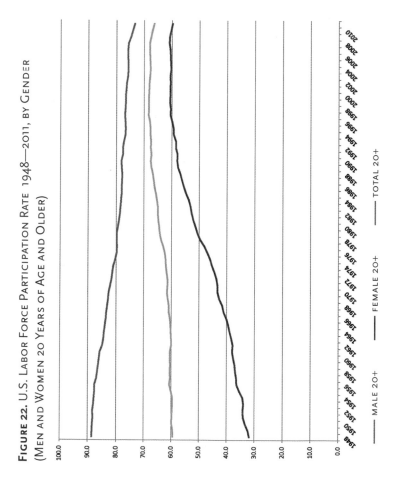

FIGURE 22. U.S. LABOR FORCE PARTICIPATION RATE 1948—2011, BY GENDER (MEN AND WOMEN 20 YEARS OF AGE AND OLDER)

──── MALE 20+   ──── FEMALE 20+   ──── TOTAL 20+

Source: The Bureau of Labor Statistics, One Screen database, Labor Force Statistics, Series "LNU01300000,", "LNU01300001," "LNU01300002."

the past twenty years (1991–2011), for example, roughly 12 million of the country's new adult jobholders were women—but just 10 million were men.[31] A multiplicity of social changes help explain the postwar feminization of the U.S. labor force, but the great decline in work by America's men also demands notice and requires explanation.

Figure 23 helps us understand the phenomenon of the vanishing male worker in contemporary America. For American men twenty years of age and older, Figure 23 depicts both the employment to population ratio and the labor force participation rate. The gap between these two lines represents the unemployed; those in the workforce, seeking employment, but without jobs. As may be seen, a terrible gap between these two lines opened up in 2008, with the paroxysms of the Great Recession. At its widest level in postwar history— that is, in the year 2010—that gap amounted to 6.5 percent of the total male population ages twenty and older. On the other hand, in the sixty years between 1948 and 2008—that is to say, before the subsequent crash—the male labor force participation rate fell by nearly 13 percentage points. In other words, male employment levels today have been depressed twice as much by the drop in the share of men seeking work as by the lack of work in the depths of the Great Recession for those seeking jobs.

Between 1948 and 2011 the proportion of adult men who did not consider themselves part of the workforce steadily rose, from under 13 percent then to almost 27 percent now.

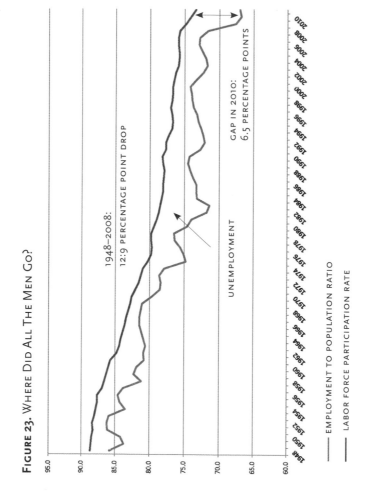

FIGURE 23. WHERE DID ALL THE MEN GO?

1948–2008:
12·9 PERCENTAGE POINT DROP

GAP IN 2010:
6.5 PERCENTAGE POINTS

UNEMPLOYMENT

EMPLOYMENT TO POPULATION RATIO
LABOR FORCE PARTICIPATION RATE

Source: The Bureau of Labor Statistics, One Screen database, Labor Force Statistics, Series "LNU01300001," and "LNS12300001."

From this perspective, it would appear that a large part of the jobs problem for American men today is that of not wanting one.

The decline in male labor force participation rates since the end of World War II admittedly does reflect in part the aging of American society. But that particular aspect of the overarching postwar male flight from work should not be overstated. In 1950, men age sixty-five or older comprised just under 12 percent of all men above the age of twenty;[32] sixty years later, the corresponding figure was just under 16 point drop.[33] Thus the growth in the share of senior citizens can only explain at most 4 percent of the drop in labor force participation rates for men (on the extreme and counterfactual presumption that no men over 65 work), only a small portion of the total 16 percent. More consequential was the retreat from work in the prime working-age groups. In 1950 just 3.5 percent of noninstitutionalized American men between the ages of twenty-five and fifty-four did not count themselves as part of the country's workforce. Sixty years later, the corresponding share was over three times as high—almost 11 percent.[34] In the intervening years, incidentally, the health status of that twenty-five- to fifty-four-year-old group improved substantially: where the odds of dying during that portion of the life course was about 19 percent for American men back in 1950, it has dropped to less than 9 percent by 2009.[35]

Americans still tend to regard themselves as a distinctively hard-working people, and in important respects, hard facts do bear this out. Americans with jobs work much longer nowadays than their continental European counterparts: by the reckoning of Harvard's Alberto Alesina and his colleagues, in the early years of the 2000s, employed Americans were working an average of more than eighteen hundred hours per year—20 to 25 percent longer than the average German or French worker, 35 percent longer than the average for Sweden, and almost 50 percent longer than counterparts in the Netherlands.[36] But these averages are for people actually at work. Paradoxically, labor force participation ratios for men in the prime of life are demonstrably *lower* in America than in Europe today.

The paradox is highlighted in Figure 24, which contrasts labor force participation rates for men in their late thirties in the United States and Greece. In the United States, as in most modern societies, men in their late thirties are the demographic group within society with the very highest rates of labor force participation. And Greece, given its ongoing public debt and finance travails, is at the moment a sort of poster child for the over-bloated, unsustainable European welfare state. Be all that as it may: the fact is that a decidedly *smaller* share of men in their late thirties has apparently opted out of the workforce in Greece than in the United States. By 2003—well before the Great Recession—7.2 percent of American men in this age group were outside the workforce, as against just 3 percent in Greece. Nor is Greece an anomalous representative of European work patterns in this regard. Quite the contrary: According to the International Labor Office's LABORSTA database,[37] almost every Western European society was maintaining higher labor force participation rates than America by this criterion. Indeed, around the year 2004, thirteen members of the EU-15 reported higher participation rates for men in their late thirties than America's own (only Sweden's was a shade lower—Britain's data, for their part, do not break out participation rates for the thirty-five- to thirty-nine-year-old age group). Europeans may take a great many holidays and vacations to the American eye—but the fact of the matter is that American men near the height of their powers are much more likely than their European brethren to go on *permanent vacation*.

How has America's great postwar male flight from work been possible? To ask the question is to answer it. This is a creature of our entitlement society and could not have been possible without it. Transfers for retirement, income maintenance, unemployment insurance, and all the rest have made it possible for a lower fraction of adult men to be engaged in work today than at any time since the Great Depression—and, quite possibly, at any previous point in our national history.

For American men, work is no longer a duty or a necessity; rather, it is an option. In making work merely optional for America's men, the U.S. entitlement state has undermined the foundations of what earlier generations termed "the manly

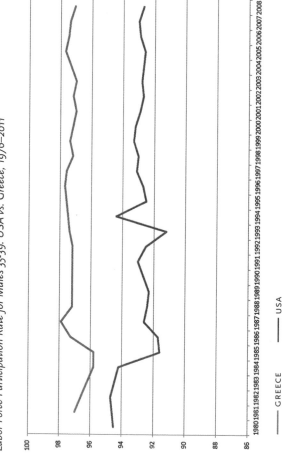

FIGURE 24. THOSE HARD WORKING GREEKS . . .
Labor Force Participation Rate for Males 35-39: USA vs. Greece, 1976–2011

GREECE ——   USA ——

Sources: The Bureau of Labor Statistics, One Screen database, Labor Force Statistics, Series "LNU01300001."

International Labor Office: Economically Active Population, Greece, 1948–2008.

virtues"—unapologetically, and without irony. Whatever else may be said about our country's earlier gender roles and stereotypes, it was the case the manly virtues cast able-bodied men as protectors of society, not predators living off of it. That much can no longer be said.

From a Nation of Takers to a Nation of Gamers to a Nation of Chiselers

With the disappearance of the historical stigma against dependence on government largesse, and the normalization of lifestyles relying upon official resource transfers, it is not surprising that ordinary Americans should have turned their noted entrepreneurial spirit not simply to maximizing their take from the existing entitlement system, but to extracting payouts from the transfer state that were never intended under its programs. In this environment, gaming and defrauding the entitlement system have emerged as a mass phenomenon in modern America, a way of life for millions upon millions of men and women who would no doubt unhesitatingly describe themselves as law-abiding and patriotic American citizens.

Abuse of the generosity of our welfare state has, to be sure, aroused the ire of the American public in the past, and continues to arouse it from time to time today. For decades, a special spot in the rhetorical public square has been reserved for pillorying unemployed "underclass" gamers who cadge undeserved social benefits. (This is the "welfare Cadillac" trope, and its many coded alternatives.) Public disapproval of this particular variant of entitlement misuse was sufficiently strong that Congress managed in the mid-1990s to overhaul the notorious AFDC program in a reform of welfare that replaced the old structure with Temporary Assistance for Needy Families (TANF). But entitlement fiddling in modern America is by no means the exclusive preserve of a troubled underclass. Quite the contrary: it is today characteristic of working America, and even those who would identify themselves as middle class.

Exhibit A in the documentation of widespread entitlement abuse in mainstream America is the explosion over the past half-century of disability claims and awards under the disability insurance provisions of the U.S. Social Security program. In 1960 an average of 455,000 erstwhile workers were receiving monthly federal payments for disability. By 2010 that total had skyrocketed to 8.2 million (and by 2011 had risen still further, to almost 8.6 million).[38] Thus, the number of Americans collecting government disability payments soared eighteen-fold over the fifty years from 1960 and 2010. In the early 1960s almost twice as many adults were receiving AFDC checks as disability payments;[39] by 2010, disability payees outnumbered the average calendar-year TANF caseload by more than four to one (8.20 million vs. 1.86 million[40]). Moreover, "workers" who were recipients of government disability payments had jumped from the equivalent of 0.65 percent of the economically active eighteen- to sixty-four-year-old population in 1960 to 5.6 percent by 2010. In 1960, there were over 150 men and women in those age groups working or seeking employment for every person on disability; by 2010, the ratio was 18 to 1 and continuing to decrease. The ratios are even starker when it comes to paid work: in 1960, roughly 134 Americans were engaged in gainful employment for every officially disabled worker; by December 2010 there were just over 16.[41] And by some measures, the situation today looks even more unfavorable than this.[42]

Although the Social Security Administration does not publish data on the ethnicity of its disability payees, it does publish information on a state-by-state basis. These suggest that the proclivity to rely upon government disability payments today is at least as much a "white thing" as a tendency for any other American group. As of December 2011 the state with the very highest ratio of working-age disability awardees to the resident population ages eighteen to sixty-four was West Virginia (9.0 percent—meaning that every eleventh adult in this age group was on paid government disability). According to Census Bureau estimates, 93 percent of West Virginia's population was "non-Hispanic white" in 2011.[43] In New England, by the same token, all-but-lily-white Maine (where ethnic minorities accounted for less than 6 percent of the population[44] in 2011) records a 7.4 percent ratio of working-age disability payees to resident working-age population: more than one out of fourteen.

On the other hand, in the District of Columbia, where

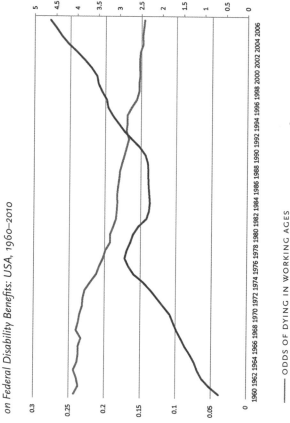

FIGURE 25. What Is Wrong with This Picture?
Odds of Dying between Ages 18 and 65 vs. Percentage of Labor Force Ages 18–64 on Federal Disability Benefits: USA, 1960–2010

ODDS OF DYING IN WORKING AGES

DISABILITY TO TOTAL PEOPLE AGES 18–64 IN LABOR FORCE (PERCENT)

Source: Mortality Rates: The Human Mortality Database, lx.

Disability Rates: Social Security Administration, Office of Retirement and Disability Policy, Annual Statistical Report on the Social Security Disability Insurance Program, 2010.

Labor Force: The Bureau of Labor Statistics, One Screen database, Labor Force Statistics, Series "LNU01300001."

so-called Anglos or non-Hispanic whites composed just 35 percent of the population in 2011,[45] the ratio of working-age disability recipients to working-age resident population was 3.3 percent—less than half of Maine's, and bit more than a third of West Virginia's.

America's dramatic long-term rise in the proportion of working-age men and women designated as possessing entitlement-worthy disabilities is all the more remarkable when one bears in mind the tremendous improvements in public health between 1960 and 2010. Between 1960 and 2009, according to the reckoning of the Human Mortality Database, overall life expectancy at birth in the United States increased by nearly nine years, and life expectancy at age eighteen jumped by seven years (from 54.5 to 61.5). Over that same period, the odds of dying between one's eighteenth and sixty-fifth birthdays fell markedly: from 26.1 percent to 15.1 percent, or by well over two-fifths[46] (see Figure 25). Furthermore, the automation of work and the rise of the service/information economy over those same decades made the daily routines of Americans ever less physically demanding. Given these factors, what's the source of the seven-fold rise in the proportion of working-age Americans on government-paid disability over the past half-century?

Paradoxically, despite the general aging of the population as a whole and the workforce in particular, there has been a gradual *reduction* in the age of the disability-entitled over time.[47] In 1960, for example, 6.6 percent of men and 6.4

percent of women on disability were in their 30s or early 40s; by 2011 the corresponding shares were 15 percent and 16.2 percent, respectively.[48] More and more Americans, it would seem, are making the securing of disability status their life-long career. Collecting disability is an increasingly important "profession" in America these days.

Hints can be found in the diagnostic categories under which disability claimants were awarded their federal stipends. In December 2011, of the 8.6 million workers on OASD disability, 1.5 million, or slightly over 15 percent, were granted on the basis of "mood disorders," and another 2.5 million, or 29 percent, for diseases of the "musculoskeletal system and the connective tissue."[49] Together, these diagnoses make up nearly half of all disability diagnoses today. In 1960, in contrast, musculoskeletal problems and mental disorders of all types accounted for only one-fifth of disability awards.[50]

The exceptionally rapid increase in awards for mood disorders and musculoskeletal problems over the past fifty-plus years may speak in part to improvements in diagnostics and redress of previously unreported afflictions. On the other hand, one may note that it is exceptionally difficult—for all practical purposes, impossible—for a medical professional to *disprove* a patient's claim that he or she is suffering from sad feelings or back pain.

By year-end 2011, more Americans were "employed" (in the sense of having a source of steady income) via government disability than from construction, or transport and warehousing, and over three times as many as in information technology services. In terms of gross manpower, workers on disability pay are today nearly in the same league as the entire U.S. manufacturing sector: for every one hundred industrial workers in December 2010, there were seventy-three "workers" receiving OASDI pay—and in that same year more Americans of working age were getting disability checks from some government program than from any U.S. manufacturer.

Apparently, disability is also the healthiest and most dynamic area of the labor force. In the two years between January 2010 and December 2011, for example, the U.S. economy generated 1.73 million nonfarm jobs—but added almost half as many (790,000) workers to the roll of federal disability payments. Nor can this perverse pattern be discounted as a short-term phenomenon peculiar to the nature of the recovery from the crash of 2008. Over the fifteen years between December 1996 and December 2011, America gained 8.8 million nonfarm private-sector jobs—and 4.1 million workers on disability payment. In the decade between December 2001 and December 2011, nongovernment nonfarm employment rose by fewer than 1 million jobs (828,000), while the ranks of the working-disabled swelled by over 3 million (3.036 million).

In FY 2011 the Social Security Administration disbursed over $130 billion in payments for its Disability Insurance (DI) program. An additional $56 billion went to the Supplemental

Security Income (SSI) program, many of whose recipients qualify on the grounds of being work-disabled.[51] Many more claimants are taking benefits from the DI program today than was envisioned by its overseers even a few years ago. According to recent projections by the Congressional Budget Office, the Social Security DI trust fund is on track to go bankrupt in just four years.[52] The greatest costs from the mass gaming of disability payments, however, are not necessarily economic.

In "playing" the disability system, or cheating it outright, many millions of Americans are making a living by putting their hands into the pockets of their fellow citizen—be they taxpayers now alive or as yet unborn (a steadily growing phenomenon, as we shall see in a moment). And it is not simply the disability gamers themselves who are complicit in this modern scam. The army of doctors and health-care professionals who are involved in, and paid for their services in, certifying dubious workers' compensation cases are direct—indeed indispensable—collaborators in the operation. The U.S. judicial system—which rules on disability cases and sets the standards for disability qualification—is likewise compromised. More fundamentally, American voters and their elected representatives are ultimately responsible for this state of affairs, as its willing and often knowing enablers. This popular tolerance for widespread dishonesty at the demonstrable expense of fellow citizens leads to an impoverishment of the country's civic spirit and an incalculable degradation of the nation's constituting principles.

The Myth of "Pay-as-You-Go" Entitlements: In Reality, Increasingly Financed by the Unborn

As Americans opt to reward themselves ever more lavishly with entitlement benefits, the question of how to pay for these government transfers inescapably comes to the fore. As the transfer payment lifestyle has become normalized and generalized in modern America, the American public has become ever more broadminded about the propriety of tapping new sources of finance for supporting their appetite for more, immediate entitlements. Thus the taker mentality has thus ineluctably gravitated toward taking from a pool of citizens who can offer no resistance to such schemes: the unborn descendants of today's entitlement-seeking population.

The intention to plunder the earnings of future generations of Americans through current entitlement programs is, at least for now, most transparent in the design of our policies for income maintenance and health care for our retirees and older citizens: namely, Social Security (more technically, it's "Old Age Social Insurance" or OASI subcomponent) and Medicare. In theory, Social Security and Medicare are both meant to be self-financed social insurance programs, by which an enrollee's premium payments during the working years cover needs in retirement and later life. Thus the political mantra, embraced by both parties today, that Social Security and Medicare are not entitlement programs but rather "social insurance" projects. Yet the uncomfortable reality of these entitlement arrangements is very different from this notion.

As actually structured, these programs have never actually attempted the self-finance of eventual benefits by payroll taxes from working contributors.[53] Rather, they rely upon contributions from current workers to sustain current recipients. Those arrangements are known as the "pay-as-you-go" approach. And although Social Security and Medicare beneficiaries formally draw their payments from officially established trust funds, as a practical matter these outlays are not meant to be paid for through set-asides from the recipient cohorts themselves (though Medicare has been in operation for over forty-five years, and Social Security over seventy-five years). Instead they are designed to rely upon the resources of subsequent cohorts of income earners. In effect, both are intergenerational resource transfer plans, whereby today's takers, with very few exceptions, consume at the expense of those born after them.

Under such circumstances, it may seem like only a small step to move from taxing the current generation of workers to the following generation—or untold ones after that—in order to provide today's older Americans with the government pensions and health care services they take as their due. That fateful line was crossed by the U.S. welfare state long ago: there has never been any great interest in protecting of the rights of the unborn on the part of U.S. social insurance programs and their presumptive beneficiaries. In consequence, all too predictably, the U.S. trust funds for both Social Security–OASI and Medicare are not endowments at all, but accounting contrivances built upon a mountain of future IOUs.

The plain fact is that neither the Social Security nor the Medicare trust funds can honor the future promises they have made today. Both are woefully unsound from an actuarial standpoint, which is no secret. The administrators of both entitlement programs not only admit as much, but calculate the estimated magnitude of these unpayable promises (the "net present value of unfunded liabilities") every year in a report to the respective funds' trustees.

In its most recent report the Social Security program reckons these unfunded liabilities to be on the order of $8.6 trillion current U.S. dollars for the seventy-five years commencing January 1, 2012. If the program is to last indefinitely, the implied "unfunded liability through an infinite horizon" would be over $20 trillion.[54] By way of comparison, at the start of 2012, the U.S. GDP amounted to a little over $15 trillion.[55]

The Medicare program, for its part, may be even further out of kilter. The 2012 Medicare trustee's report indicates its unfunded obligations over the next seventy-five years to total nearly $27 trillion,[56] and this assessment may be optimistic as an alternative scenario offered by Medicare's Office of the Actuary presented an outlook of nearly $37 trillion in unfunded obligations over those same years.[57] Some careful independent analysts have suggested that the true size of these unfunded liabilities may be still greater than the government's actuaries suggest.[58] (And the "infinite horizon" estimate of Medicare's unfunded liabilities would presumably be still larger.)

These calculations are, of course, subject to technical considerations and assumptions (the growth outlook, the demographic outlook, the suitable long-term interest rate, the cost outlook for goods and services inside and outside the health sector, and so forth). Their results, accordingly, are sensitive to changes in assumptions about the future. They are thus best regarded as ballpark projections rather than precise forecasts.

Such computational arcana, however, should not distract from the central driver behind these truly stupendous imbalances underlying our two largest entitlement programs: the impulse to take benefits here and now, and leave it to other people later on to figure out how to pay for it all. There are many possible rationalizations for such a disposition: the notion that we have "already paid for" the old-age benefits we expect to collect through our past payroll taxes (a patent arithmetic misconception), for example, or the notion that our descendants will likely be more affluent than we are and thus better set than we are to take care of the bills we are leaving behind for them. Yet whatever the rationalizations—and a great many of them circulate in public discourse today— none can make up for the sacrifice of principle that lies at the heart of this problem. For the sake of pure short-term expedience, the U.S. democracy has decided to mortgage its tomorrow for a more comfortable retirement today.

To some, the question of the unfunded balances in our very biggest entitlement programs may seem abstract, or even moot. The future, after all, is full of incertitudes, and a world seventy-five years hence is hard to envision with any confidence. The here and now, on the other hand, is all too real and pressing, too. Politics, as a sport played on a day-by-day basis, is especially responsive to immediate desires and urges. Yet the consequences of the increasing American fiscal predilection for using the unborn as a sort of all-purpose credit card are already coming into view.

As much may be seen in Figure 26, which contraposes government outlays for Social Security and Medicare against the federal budget deficit over the past four decades. There is an irregular but all too steady correspondence between those two quantities over the years in question. The federal deficit is an arithmetic difference between receipts and expenditures, and thus not program-specific. Yet to judge only by its performance specifics, one would be tempted to say that the purpose of the federal deficit in recent decades has in effect been to fund our pay-as-you-go entitlement programs. (This was not true in the mid- to late 1990s, in the years when the Clinton presidency was squaring off against a Republican Congress—but those years in retrospect look like a temporary aberration.) In recent years, the federal deficit has been

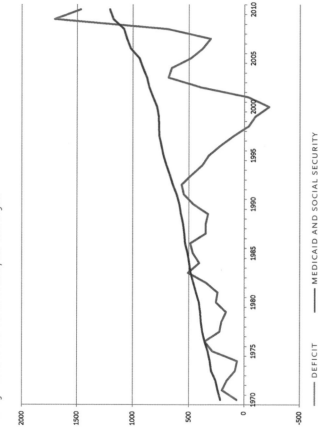

FIGURE 26. WHO PAYS FOR THESE ENTITLEMENTS?
Cost of Medicare and Social Security vs. U.S. Deficit

Sources: Entitlement Transfers: Bureau of Economic Analysis.

Deficit: White House Office of Management and Budget, Table 15.6- Total Government Surpluses or Deficits (-) in Absolute Amounts and as Percentages of GDP: 1948–2011.

almost exactly equal to our programmatic spending on Social Security and Medicare combined.

There are perfectly good reasons for free peoples to run government deficits and thus contract public debt: these include providing for response to dire national emergencies or perhaps underwriting investment projects in potentially productive infrastructure. The wholesale financing of current public consumption through the device of obliging unborn Americans to cover those costs (plus interest), however, has not previously been characteristic of our democratic governance.[59] Irrespective of the economic implications of this insidious innovation, this new approach to entitlements necessarily means we will be leaving a very different heritage of mores to our legatees from the one that we inherited from our forebears.

CROWDING OUT DEFENSE: MAKING NATIONAL SECURITY "UNAFFORDABLE" FOR HISTORY'S RICHEST COUNTRY

Unlike entitlement payments which are nowhere mentioned in the Constitution (and might even have been unimaginable to our Founding Fathers as a function of government), the U.S. Constitution expressly establishes national security, and the maintenance of the armed forces to provide for "our common defense," as a prime responsibility for the American state. Recall, perhaps, that the president's first (and thus foremost) enumerated power under the Constitution is in his role as "commander in chief" (Article II, Section 2).

Over the past generations, that task of providing for the common defense was acquitted tolerably well. For better or worse, the United States in fact ended up as the world's sole superpower at the dawn of the new millennium (at least for the time being), having won, *inter alia*, two world wars and a cold war. As one might expect from such exertions, American defense has been a staggeringly expensive project over the past century. At this writing (2012), overall national defense expenditures are running at over $700 billion a year[60]—a level that not only dwarfs any other presumptive contemporary competitor, but accounts for close to half of all worldwide military expenditures, according to many analysts.[61]

The size and scope of America's military allocations, to be sure, has many critics—at home as well as abroad. Commentators on the right and left of the U.S. political spectrum decry what they call the American "national security state" (a term that has acquired a marked opprobrium in the decades since its early and decidedly more neutral Cold War coinage). And concern about excessive defense spending has hardly been a preserve of fringe extremists. No less a figure than Dwight Eisenhower, architect of the D-Day invasion and onetime supreme commander of NATO forces, warned of the dangers of a "military-industrial complex" in his famous 1961 farewell presidential address.[62]

A healthy measure of informed public skepticism toward

any and all proposed military expenditures is not only suitable but essential for open democratic societies. A free people, after all, will jealously guard against impingements upon their liberties—including those arising from excessive, wasteful, or unwise outlays in the name of national defense.

But the notion that defense spending today is entirely or even mainly accountable for the burden of government that the American citizenry shoulders, though still widely believed, is by now utterly antique and completely at odds with the most basic current facts. The days in which the national security state arrogated more public resources than the welfare state are long past. U.S. government outlays on entitlements do not merely exceed those for defense nowadays, they completely overshadow defense outlays. Increasingly, moreover, our seemingly insatiable national hunger for government transfer payments to individual citizens stand to compromise our present and future capabilities for military readiness.

In 1961, the year of Eisenhower's admonition about the military-industrial complex, America was devoting close to two dollars on defense for every dollar it provided in domestic entitlement payments.[63] Up to that point, defense expenditures had routinely exceeded any and all allocations for social insurance and social welfare throughout American history.[64] But in 1961 a geometric growth of entitlement payments was just commencing. Thanks to the unrelenting force of that spending surge, government transfer payments to individuals would surpass defense spending in just a decade—in

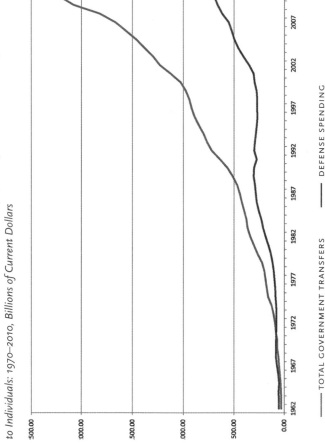

FIGURE 27. CROWDING OUT DEFENSE *Military Spending vs. Government Transfers to Individuals: 1970–2010, Billions of Current Dollars*

TOTAL GOVERNMENT TRANSFERS   DEFENSE SPENDING

Sources: Transfers: Bureau of Economic Analysis.

Military Spending: White House Office of Management and Budget, Historical Tables, Table 3.2, Outlays by Function and Subfunction.

1971, in the midst of the Vietnam War. And for the following forty years, entitlements have continued to surpass defense expenditures—by progressively widening margins. By the year 2010 America was spending well over three times as much on transfer payments as on its entire national security budget—notwithstanding active and simultaneous overseas military campaigns in Iraq and Afghanistan (see Figure 27).

America's ramp-up of military outlays in the decade after the September 11, 2001, attacks is well known. Much less widely known is the fact that this massive upsurge in military spending was more or less eclipsed by the enormous increase in spending on domestic entitlements over those same years. This fact may be demonstrated in many different ways, but a comparison of current spending trends for defense and entitlements over the 2001–10 period of time may be clearest.[65]

In FY 2001 the United States spent $305 billion on defense; for 2001–10, the cumulative total was $5.05 trillion. Over those ten years, in other words, America spent $2 trillion more on defense than if it had just continued along at the 2001 baseline. In contrast, America was spending $1.13 trillion on entitlements in 2001, and ended up spending a cumulative total of $16.03 trillion on those transfers for 2001–10. This was nearly $4.8 trillion more than would have been spent on the nominal dollar baseline from 2001. By this measure, the absolute growth over the last decade in entitlement spending was nearly two and a half times greater than the corresponding increment in defense spending. The magnitude of the upsurge in military spending over those years was widely discussed over those same years, and often decried as being "unaffordable." Curiously, considering the magnitude of the quantities involved, the great simultaneous leap in entitlement spending did not seem to attract similar critical public attention.

At this writing, the U.S. defense budget is under mounting pressure. It is more than just a matter of winding down America's commitments in Iraq and Afghanistan; a much more fundamental and far-reaching recasting of defense posture and global capabilities appears to be afoot. Its gathering manifestations are seen in the 2012 White House budget request, which slashed nearly half a trillion dollars from the previous official plans for military spending over the coming decade, and from the president's January 2012 strategic guidance to revise and downsize America's global force structure.[66] And these cuts may only be a foretaste of what is to come: last year's bipartisan congressional "sequestration" deal, for example, calls for another half trillion dollars in prospective defense cuts in the years immediately ahead if a deficit reduction deal is not hammered out by the end of 2012.

The rationale for the slashing of overall U.S. defense capabilities in the years ahead is spelled out plainly in the Defense Department's document on the new policy: budgetary exigency. As the president's transmittal letter puts it, "We must put our fiscal house in order and renew our long-term economic strength. To that end, the Budget Control Act of 2011 (the aforementioned 'sequestration' deal) mandates

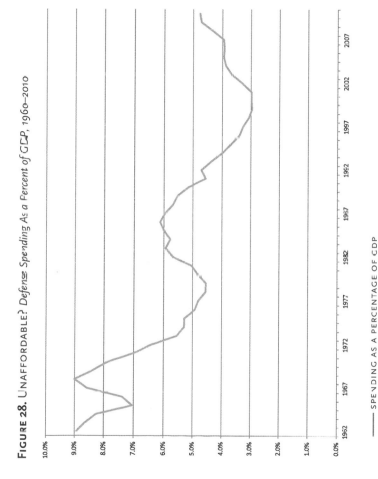

FIGURE 28. UNAFFORDABLE? *Defense Spending As a Percent of GDP, 1960–2010*

Sources: Spending: White House Office of Management and Budget, Historical Tables, Table 3.2, Outlays by Function and Subfunction.

GDP: Bureau of Economic Analysis.

reductions in federal spending, including defense spending."[67] In short, America's current defense posture is unsustainable because it is unaffordable.

But why, exactly, should America's current and (heretofore) future military commitments be regarded as "unaffordable"?

In 2010 the national defense budget amounted to 4.8 percent of current GDP (see Figure 28). As a fraction of U.S. national output, our military burden was thus lower in 2010 than in almost any year during the four-plus decades of the Cold War era. In 1961—the year of Eisenhower's "military industrial complex" address—the ratio of defense spending to GDP was 9.4 percent[68]; in other words, almost twice as high as in 2010. Put another way: America's overall military burden was nearly twice as high in 1961 as in 2010. Americans may have deemed our defense commitments in 2010 to be ill-advised, poorly purchased, or otherwise of questionable provenance—but as a pure question of affordability, the United States is in a better position to afford our current defense burden than at virtually any time during the Cold War era.

The true problem with defense "affordability" today is not our ability to pay for these outlays per se, but rather our overall national spending priorities. Entitlements are still sacrosanct; there is as yet no serious talk of reigning in their growth path. The aforementioned congressional sequestration deal does not dare to cut into any of this group of outlays—nor does the president's new budget proposal. By the calculus of

American policymakers today then, U.S. defense capabilities seem to be the primary area sacrificed to make the world safe for the unrestrained growth of American entitlements.

But this inverted, perverse, and feckless mind-set can only take a nation of takers so far, notwithstanding all that this approach may presage for the security of our country. As a matter of pure arithmetic, the urge to skimp on national defense to support our welfare state is utterly unsustainable. Consider this. On its current trajectory, the U.S. government's transfer payments are on track to increase by over $700 billion over the next four years. As it happens, our total current national outlay for all defense and security programs is roughly $700 billion. Even if our national defenses were to be eliminated totally tomorrow, it would at this juncture take just one presidential term for the growth of personal transfers from the U.S. government to absorb the totality of our entire current defense budget.

ENTITLEMENTS, DEPENDENCE, AND THE POLITICS OF POPULIST REDISTRIBUTION

An unavoidable consequence of the noxious something-for-nothing thinking that lies at the heart of the modern entitlement mentality is the resort to redistributionist politics. Actuarially sound insurance programs are one thing, but if we are to count on drawing more from the public purse than we can predictably be said to have contributed, someone else

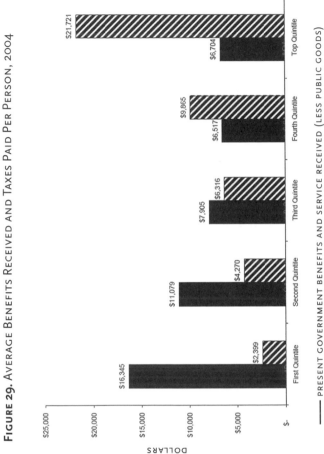

FIGURE 29. AVERAGE BENEFITS RECEIVED AND TAXES PAID PER PERSON, 2004

— PRESENT GOVERNMENT BENEFITS AND SERVICE RECEIVED (LESS PUBLIC GOODS)

▓ TAXES AND REVENUES PAID

First Quintile: $16,345 / $2,399
Second Quintile: $11,079 / $4,270
Third Quintile: $7,905 / $6,316
Fourth Quintile: $9,865 / $6,517
Top Quintile: $21,721 / $6,704

Source: Robert Rector and Christine Kim, "How the Wealth is Spread: The Distribution of Government Benefits, Services and Taxes by Income Quintile in the United States," Fall 2008 Conference of The Association for Public Policy Analysis and Management.

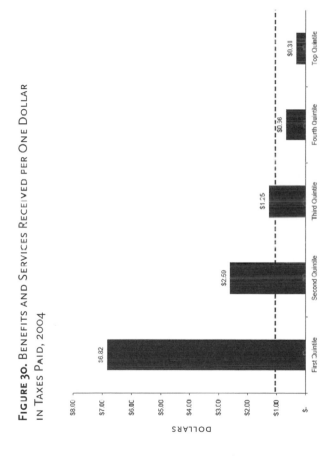

FIGURE 30. BENEFITS AND SERVICES RECEIVED PER ONE DOLLAR IN TAXES PAID, 2004

Source: Robert Rector and Christine Kim, "How the Wealth is Spread: The Distribution of Government Benefits, Services and Taxes by Income Quintile in the United States," Fall 2008 Conference of The Association for Public Policy Analysis and Management.

is going to have to foot the bill. No alternative answers are available to this simple arithmetic proposition. And today, the potential funding sources for subsidizing something-for-nothing policies are three: other countries, other citizens, or other generations. As the unwhetted contemporary public appetite for government transfers continues to mount, each of these sources will be assiduously tapped.

Plundering our descendants' wealth to finance today's entitlements is easy to do under America's current political economy—and is being done now, as already noted. Financing current entitlements from foreign wealth is a potentially feasible but decidedly more complex proposition, and it need not detain us in the context of this discussion. The final option under consideration is financing today's something-for-nothing politics from within the pool of living, voting Americans.

Curiously, very little empirical research is available on the overall incidence of taxation and transfer recipience in modern America. Available research for the most part deals with the burden of income taxes alone, excluding the many other taxes Americans bear these days—and neglecting almost entirely the issue of transfer benefits. One admirable exception to this general observation is a study by the Heritage Foundation's Robert Rector and Christine Kim, focused on the year 2004—before the Great Recession, and the calls for more redistributionist policies that crisis provoked (see Figures 29 and 30).

By Rector and Kim's estimate, U.S. fiscal policy in 2004 was highly progressive: the top fifth was transferring out a net of about $15,000 per person per year, and the bottom fifth was taking in a net of nearly $14,000 per person a year in government transfers. Poorer people paid taxes, too—to be sure. (As a study commissioned by the *Wall Street Journal* recently noted, Census Bureau data for the year 2010 indicated that only 18 percent of American household paid neither income nor payroll taxes[69]—but most of the remainder likely paid property taxes, or sales taxes, or both.) However, for every dollar in federal, state, and local taxes the top fifth gave over, they received an estimated 31 cents back in transfer benefits, whereas the bottom fifth received close to $7 in transfer benefits.

We cannot know the current landscape of redistribution until the data underlying Figure 29 is updated. Yet we do know two critical facts about the political environment that will be shaping the dynamics of political redistribution in the years immediately ahead.

The first is that earned success is being delegitimized in some political circles—including some highly powerful ones at this writing. President Obama's momentous recent campaign speech, in Roanoke, Virginia on July 13, 2012, insinuating that entrepreneurs had not achieved their own accomplishments on their own, but rather owed their wealth to preexisting government expenditures[70] on infrastructure and in their own upbringing, not only writes a narrative by which today's American wealth may be attributed to government entitlement programs, but also opens the rhetorical door to almost limitless extractions from the well-to-do on the grounds that their success is not really theirs to enjoy.

The second would be the brute facts of rising calendar-year income dispersion in modern America, and seemingly ever greater year-to-year volatility in household earnings.[71] With more or less steadily rising "income inequality" by such metrics (though not by all metrics regarding economic inequality[72]) the call may gradually grow for explicitly redistributionist policies—whether to redress purportedly embedded structural defaults in our economic system, or to stimulate prosperity through neo-Keynesian spending schemes, or both.

The underlying problem here, unfortunately, is that such battle cries are in themselves subversive of both the formula that has to date facilitated such an extraordinary generation of wealth in the American republic and its moral underpinnings. Something-for-nothing politics requires at least a pretense of justification for its takings, and one of the most convenient rationales for excusing such takings is the claim that our opportunity society no longer really works. The irony here is that something-for-nothing politics can itself make the claim come true—if pursued on a sufficiently grand scale and in a sufficiently reckless manner.

A NATION OF TAKERS:
IS THE SYNDROME UNSUSTAINABLE?

Within policymaking circles in Washington today, observing that America's national hunger for entitlement benefits has placed the country on a financially untenable trajectory, with the federal budget—which is to say, the entitlements machine—generating ultimately unbearable expenditures and levels of public debt is very close to received wisdom. The bipartisan 2010 Bowles/Simpson Commission put the viewpoint plainly: "Our nation is on an unsustainable fiscal path."[73] The same point has been made by many in Congress, by the Congressional Budget Office (CBO), and by the current head of the President's Council of Economic Advisers (CEA), who wrote an academic paper shortly before entering the government warning that projections by the CBO and the trust funds for Social Security and Medicare were likely much too optimistic, that fiscal imbalances were on track to pose a public debt crisis within a decade, and that avoiding such a crisis would "require much larger changes than have received serious consideration in the policy process to date."[74]

The prospect of careening along an unsustainable economic road is deeply disturbing. But another possibility is even more frightening—namely, that the present course may in fact be sustainable for far longer than most people today might imagine.

The United States is a very wealthy society. If it so chooses, it has vast resources to liquidate. In the public sphere are many trillions of dollars worth of assets, accumulated over the centuries—land, buildings, art, and the like—that can still be sold. In the private sector, corporate and personal debt still exceeds net public debt by a very healthy ratio. According to the Federal Reserve Bank's estimate, as of 2011, three-quarters of all U.S. credit market debt had been contracted for private purposes (mortgages, business investments, and the like).[75] Thus there remains plenty of room for diminishing the role of such transactions in American economic life—or perhaps for crowding them out almost altogether.

The U.S. dollar is still the world's reserve currency, so there is plenty of scope for taking financial advantage of that privilege. As a practical matter, there is no realistic international alternative to the dollar—at least for now. It could take many years—maybe decades—for the United States to sacrifice this status by undermining the dollar's credibility as an international medium of exchange.[76] Debasing the dollar to finance continuing expansion of domestic spending could eventually look like an option worthy of serious consideration—at least, in an America addicted to and enslaved by entitlements.

Such devices could indefinitely forestall economic ruin—but they might well greatly postpone the day of judgment. Not so the credibility of the American character: that would be lost long before the credibility of the U.S. economy. Some would argue that asset is already wasting away before our very eyes.

Notes

1. Daniel Patrick Moynihan, *The Politics of a Guaranteed Income* (New York: Random House, 1973), 17.
2. Bureau of Economic Analysis, State Personal Income 2005, Section VI: Personal Current Transfer Receipts, March 28, 2006, http://www.bea.gov/regional/pdf/spi2005/06%20Personal%20Current%20Transfer%20Receipts.pdf.
3. *Merriam-Webster.com*, s.v. "entitlement," http://www.merriam-webster.com/entitlement.

4. Derived from Bureau of Economic Analysis, Regional Data, State and Personal Income, Selected Data: SA35—Personal current transfer receipts, http://www.bea.gov/iTable/iTable.cfm?ReqID=70&step=1, and Bureau of Economic Analysis, Regional Data, GDP & Personal Income, Selected Data: SA1-3 Personal income summary, http://www.bea.gov/iTable/iTable.cfm?ReqID=70&step=1.

5. These calculations use the Consumer Price Index (CPI) to adjust for inflation. See U.S. Department of Labor, Bureau of Labor Statistics, Consumer Price Index, ftp://ftp.bls.gov/pub/special.requests/cpi/cpiai.txt. A good technical argument can be made for using the Personal Consumption Expenditure Price Index (PCEPI) instead. PCEPI series available at Bureau of Economic Analysis, National Data, National Income and Product Accounts, Interactive Data, Table 2.8.4. Price Indexes for Personal Consumption Expenditures by Major Type of Product, Monthly, http://www.bea.gov/iTable/iTable.cfm?ReqID=9&step=1. Using the PCEPI, the real growth of entitlement transfers would have been over fifteen-fold, an average annual pace of 5.6 percent.

6. Using the PCEPI, the tempo would have been closer to 4.4 percent per annum, implying a total increase of about 860 percent.

7. Bureau of Economic Analysis, Personal Income and Outlays, Table 2.1, Personal Income and Its Disposition http://www.bea.gov/iTable/iTable.cfm?reqid=9&step=3&isuri=1&910=X&911=0&903=58&904=1929&905=2012&906=A.

8. Central Intelligence Agency, *The CIA World Factbook 2012* (New York: Skyhorse Publishing, 2012), 233, 332, 691. By these estimates, the 2010 official exchange rate based GDP for Italy was $2.06 trillion; for Britain, $2.25 trillion; and for France, $2.58 trillion. By this yardstick, France, Britain, and Italy were the planet's fifth, sixth and seventh largest economies at the time (outranked only by Germany, Japan, China and the United States itself).

9. Bureau of Economic Analysis, Survey of Current Business, vol. 9, no. 8, August 2011, GDP and Other Major NIPA Series, 1929–2011:II, http://www.bea.gov/scb/pdf/2011/08%20August/0811_gdp_nipas.pdf.

10. Note, however, that Social Security payments do not only accrue to older Americans. The Social Security Trust Fund's Old Age and Survivors Insurance (OASI) program, which dispenses the overwhelming majority of Social Security outlays, is indeed an age-related entitlement

program, but Social Security also encompasses a Disability Insurance (DI) program and a Supplemental Security Income (SSI) program, whose benefits are not restricted to older Americans but are instead devoted primarily to disability claims. We will discuss disability entitlements later in this book.

11. For the statistically inclined: a simple analysis shows that the real (CPI adjusted) trend for entitlement spending from 1960–2010 was 4.5 percent growth per year—and the value for a "dummy variable" for a Republican in the White House was significant at the $p<0.05$ level and indicated an increase in spending of 9.3 percent above what would be expected from the annual trendline. This simple equation garnered a r-square of 0.95, meaning that it could "predict" 95 percent of the year-to-year change in real entitlement spending over that half century.

    Of course Congress also has a role in the path of entitlements. Statistical analysis, however, did not reveal any meaningful (i.e., "statistically significant") correspondences between spending trends and the party in charge of Congress over this period (although spending does looks to have been slightly higher when Democrats were in charge of both House and Senate).

12. Estimates by the late economic historian Angus Maddison make the point. By his reckoning, real per capita GDP in America in 1890 was just 11 percent of the pre-crisis 2008 level; in 1830; barely 4 percent the 2008 level.

13. A succinct and highly informative overview of American poverty and social welfare policy from Colonial times to the present day may be found in Price V. Fishback, editor, "Social Insurance and Public Assistance," Chapter Bf, in Susan B. Carter, et al., editors, *Historical Statistics of the United States, Millennial Edition* (New York: Cambridge University Press, 2006), 2–719.

14. At much the same time, it was learned that EBT spending could no longer be demonstrably limited to food purchase. In practice, the government apparently no longer tries to account for the purposes for which these debit cards are used. See Luke Rosiak, "Top Secret: Feds Won't Say What Food Stamps Buy," *Washington Times*, June 24, 2012, http://times247.com/articles/top-secret-feds-give-80b-a-year-in-food-stamps-but-won-t-reveal-what-s-purchased.mobile.

15. Michael D. Shear, "'Julia' Becomes Vehicle for Obama's Messag-

ing," *The New York Times' The Caucus*, May 3, 2012. See http://the caucus.blogs.nytimes.com/2012/05/03/julia-becomes-vehicle-for-obamas-messaging/.

16. Binyamin Appelbaum and Robert Gebeloff, "Even Critics of Safety Net Increasingly Depend on It," *The New York Times*, February 11, 2012. See http://www.nytimes.com/2012/02/12/us/even-critics-of-safety-net-increasingly-depend-on-it.html?pagewanted=1&_r=2.

17. Jeremy White, Robert Gebeloff, Ford Fessenden, Archie Tse, and Alan McLean, "The Geography of Government Benefits," *The New York Times*, February 11, 2012, See http://www.nytimes.com/interactive/2012/02/12/us/entitlement-map.html?ref=us.

18. Binyamin Appelbaum and Robert Gebeloff, "Even Critics of Safety Net Increasingly Depend on It," *The New York Times*, February 11, 2012. See http://www.nytimes.com/2012/02/12/us/even-critics-of-safety-net-increasingly-depend-on-it.html?pagewanted=6&_r=1.

19. John Ruser, Adrienne Pilot, and Charles Nelson, "Alternative Measures of Household Income: BEA Personal Income, CPS Money Income, and Beyond," Prepared for a presentation to the Federal Economic Statistics Advisory Committee on December 14, 2004. See http://www.bls.gov/bls/fesacp1061104.pdf.

20. Laura Wheaton, "Underreporting of Means-Tested Transfer Programs in the CPS and SIPP," The Urban Institute. See http://www.urban.org/UploadedPDF/411613_transfer_programs.pdf.

21. Phil Izzo, "Number of the Week: Half of U.S. Lives in Households Getting Government Benefits", Real Time Economics Blog, *Wall Street Journal,* May 29, 2012. See http://blogs.wsj.com/economics/2012/05/26/number-of-the-week-half-of-u-s-lives-in-household-getting-benefits/.

22. Readers may wonder whether the increase in entitlement recipience has been driven by the aging of the American population, since older workers are automatically guaranteed such benefits. The answer may surprise: rough calculations suggest that only about a tenth of the overall increase in the prevalence of reported entitlement recipience between the early 1980s and the Obama administration can be accounted for by the increase in America's 65-plus population. The rest has been due, in the main, to an increasing proclivity by younger households to seek and obtain entitlement benefits.

23. One may well ask why these reported rates are not 100 percent, since

virtually all Americans are eligible for Medicare and Social Security by their sixty-fifth birthday. This could in part be a matter of under-reporting, as with means-tested benefits. It is also possible that the difference could reflect the fact that some older persons wait past the age of sixty-five to collect Social Security benefits (monthly payments are scaled progressively upward for those who defer to age seventy), and some are theoretically ineligible for Medicare (such as illegal aliens who have not contributed to Social Security). Or it could be some combination of the two.

24. We should note that readily available data on U.S. entitlement program recipience reaching back over the past three decades are, strangely, not readily available from any government statistical compendium, despite the many trillions of dollars that were devoted to these pro-grams over this period. The same holds for "means tested" or "needs related" entitlements. In recent years, it has been easy to obtain data on the percentage of Americans living in homes that obtain means tested benefits (or any sort of entitlement benefit)—whereas in earlier years only data on the percentage of households obtaining such bene-fits are published. In this book we have cobbled together a trend-line from these varying sources, although there is an inescapable element of "apples versus oranges" in so doing, the exercise may nonetheless help to inform.

25. U.S. Census Bureau, 2012 Current Population Report, 60–238, Table 543: Persons Living in Households Receiving Selected Non-cash Benefits. See http://www.census.gov/compendia/statab/2012/tables/12s0543.pdf.

26. U.S. Department of Labor, Office of Policy Planning and Research, March 1965: The Negro Family–The Case for National Action. See http://www.stanford.edu/~mrosenfe/Moynihan%27s%20The%20Negro%20Family.pdf.

27. Results refer to a simple bivariate and multivariate regression with calendar year, unemployment, and family poverty rates as indepen-dent (or "x") variables and family dependency rate as the dependent (or "y") variable. R-squares for unemployment vs. family dependency and family poverty vs. family dependency were each under 0.05, and neither relationship was statistically significant; calendar year vs. fam-

ily poverty yields an R-square of 0.8 and was statistically significant. Multivariate regression with all three independent variables gave an R-square of 0.88, but produced nonsense results for family poverty (indicating that a rise in the former tended to reduce family dependence)—while offering an extraordinarily strong degree of statistical significance for the calendar-year variable, whose coefficient was 0.44 (indicating an increase in the proportion of Americans obtaining "need-related" benefits of about 4.4 percentage points per decade).

28. Daniel Patrick Moynihan, *The Politics of a Guaranteed Income* (New York: Random House, 1973), p. 18.

29. Charles Murray, *Losing Ground: American Political Society, 1950–1980* (New York: Basic Books, 1984).

30. Nicholas Eberstadt, "Economic and Material Poverty in Modern America" (unpublished paper, November 1986), p. 42. See also Michael Novak et al., *A Community of Self-Reliance: The New Consensus on Family and Welfare,* (Washington, D.C.: American Enterprise Institute, 1987), pp. 133-1334, Tables A-11 and A-12.

31. Derived from Bureau of Labor Statistics, Labor Force Statistics from the Current Population Survey, Household Data, Annual Averages: Table 2. Employment status of the civilian noninstitutional population 16 years and over by sex, 1971 to date http://www.bls.gov/cps/cpsaato2.htm.

32. Derived from U.S. Census Bureau, "Historical Statistics of the United States, Colonial Times to 1970, Part 1," Series A 119–34, 1975, p. 15.

33. Derived from U.S. Census Bureau, "Statistical Abstract of the United States: 2012," Table 9, 2012, p. 12.

34. U.S. Bureau of Labor Statistics, One Screen database, Labor Force Statistics, Series LNU01300001, http://www.bls.gov/data/.

35. Derived from life tables presented in the Human Mortality Database, University of California–Berkeley and Max Planck Institute for Demographic Research, http://www.mortality.org.

36. Alberto F. Alesina, Edward L. Glaeser, and Bruce Sacerdote, "Work and Leisure in the U.S. and Europe: Why So Different?" In Mark Gertler and Kenneth Rogoff, eds., *NBER Macroeconomic Annual 2005* (Cambridge, MA: MIT Press, 2006), Table 2 See http://www.nber.org/chapters/c0073.pdf.

37. International Labor Office Department of Statistics, LABORSTA Database, "Total and Economically Active Population by Age Group" for USA and EU-15 Countries (Austria, Belgium, Denmark, Finland, France, Germany, Greece, Ireland, Italy, Luxembourg, Netherlands, Portugal, Spain, Sweden, and United Kingdom). See http://laborsta.ilo.org/.

38. U.S. Social Security Administration, Annual Statistical Report on the Social Security Disability Insurance Program, 2011, Disabled Beneficiaries and Nondisabled Dependents, Table 1: Number, December 1960–2011, selected years. See http://www.ssa.gov/policy/docs/statcomps/di_asr/2011/sec01a.pdf.

39. Derived from *ibid.* and from Social Security Administration, Annual Statistical Supplement, 2000, Table 9.G1.—Average monthly number of recipients, total amount of cash payments, and average monthly payment, 1936–98. See http://www.socialsecurity.gov/policy/docs/statcomps/supplement/2000/9g.pdf; more precisely, the 1960 average monthly adult caseload AFDC was 1.73 times as great as the December 1960 total for workers receiving disability benefits.

40. U.S. Department of Health and Human Services, Administration for Children and Families, Office of Family Assistance, TANF: Total Number of Families, Fiscal and Calendar Year 2010 as of 05/16/2011. See http://www.acf.hhs.gov/programs/ofa/data-reports/caseload/2010/2010_family_tan.htm.

41. Derived from U.S. Social Security Administration, Annual Statistical Report on the Social Security Disability Insurance Program, 2011, Disabled Workers, Table 19. See http://www.ssa.gov/policy/docs/statcomps/di_asr/2011/sec01c.pdf; and Bureau of Labor Statistics, Labor Force Statistics from the Current Population Survey, Series LNU01000000, LNU01000086, LNU01000097, LNU02000000. See http://data.bls.gov/pdq/querytool.jsp?survey=ln. LNU02000086,LNU020000097.

42. As of December 2010, over 12.2 million beneficiaries between the ages of 18 and 64 were obtaining disability benefits from one or more Social Security sources. See U.S. Social Security Administration, Office of Retirement and Disability Policy, Facts & Figures About Social Security, 2011, Disabled Beneficiaries Aged 18–64, December 2010. See http://www.ssa.gov/policy/docs/chartbooks/fast_facts/2011/fast_facts11.html#oasdiandssi. Thus if disability payments for "workers"

from all entitlement sources (i.e., "unduplicated" totals from OASDI, SSI, etc.) were assembled into a single metric, the 2010 ratio of all disability payees to all employed workers would have been a little less than 11 to 1.

43. U.S. Department of Commerce, U.S. Census Bureau, West Virginia Quickfacts, June 7, 2012. See http://quickfacts.census.gov qfd/states/54000.html.

44. U.S. Department of Commerce, U.S. Census Bureau, Maine Quickfacts, June 7, 2012. See http://quickfacts.census.gov/qfd/states/23000.html.

45. U.S. Department of Commerce, U.S. Census Bureau, District of Columbia Quickfacts, June 7, 2012. See http://quickfacts.census.gov/qfd/states/11000.html.

46. Human Mortality Database, United States of America, Life tables (period 1x1). See http://www.mortality.org/hmd/USA/STATS/bltper_1x1.txt

47. A phenomenon noted almost two decades ago. See Kalman Rupp and David Stapleton, "Determinants of the Growth in the Social Security Administration's Disability Programs: An Overview," *Social Security Bulletin* 58, no. 4 (1995) See http://www.ssa.gov/policy/docs/ssb/v58n4/v58n4p43.pdf.

48. U.S. Social Security Administration, Annual Statistical Report on the Social Security Disability Insurance Program, 2011, Disabled Workers, Table 19. See http://www.ssa.gov/policy/docs/statcomps/di_asr/2011/sect01c.pdf.

49. U.S. Social Security Administration, Annual Statistical Report on the Social Security Disability Insurance Program, 2011, Disabled Workers, Table 24: Distribution by Diagnostic Group and Age, December 2011. See http://www.ssa.gov/policy/docs/statcomps/di_asr/2011/sect01c.pdf.

50. U.S. Social Security Administration, Annual Statistical Report on the Social Security Disability Insurance Program, 2011, Awards to Disabled Workers, Table 18: By Diagnostic Group, 1960–2000. See http://www.ssa.gov/policy/docs/statcomps/di_asr/2000/sect02b.pdf

51. U.S. Social Security Administration, FY 2013 President's Budget, Table 3: SSA Outlays by Program. See http://www.ssa.gov/budget/2013Key-Tables.pdf.

52. U.S. Congressional Budget Office, Policy Options for the Social Secu-

rity Disability Insurance Program, July 2012. See http://www.cbo. gov/sites/default/files/cbofiles/attachments/43421-DisabilityInsurance_print.pdf.

53. "When the OASI system was originally established in 1935, the original the original intent of the Roosevelt administration appears to have been to establish a pension fund with accumulated reserves, although the initial tax rate established was below the levels needed to make the fund actuarially sound. Congress and the administration abandoned this goal with the Social Security Amendment of 1939." Price V. Fishback and Melissa Thomasson, "Social Welfare: 1929 to the Present," in in Susan B. Carter, et al., editors, *Historical Statistics of the United States, Millennial Edition* (New York: Cambridge University Press, 2006), p. 2-707.

54. U.S. Social Security Administration, 2012 Old-Age, Survivors, and Disability Insurance (OASDI) Trustees Report, Table IV.B6: Unfunded OASDI Obligations through the Infinite Horizon. See http://www.ssa. gov/ oact/TR/2012/IV_B_LRest.html.

55. U.S. Bureau of Economic Analysis, News Release, June 18, 2012, Table 3; figure is for First Quarter 2012, current dollars. See http://www.bea. gov/newsreleases/national/gdp/2012/pdf/gdp1q12_3rd.pdf.

56. Joseph Antos, "Medicare's Fiscal Crisis and Options for Reform," American Enterprise Institute, April 30, 2012, 1. See http://www.aei.org/ files/2012/05/01/-antos-report-on-medicare-reform_153555880249. pdf.

57. Romina Boccia, "CBO Report Echoes Trustees on Medicare, Social Security," Heritage Foundation, June 14, 2012, Chart 4. See http://www .heritage.org/research/reports/2012/06/cbo-long-term-budget -outlook-on-the-nations-fiscal-future.

58. See, for example, Jagadeesh Gokhale and Kent Andrew Smetters, "Fiscal and Generational Imbalances: New Budget Measures for New Budget Priorities," American Enterprise Institute, August 1, 2003, which estimated the unfunded liabilities of these programs in 2003 at much higher levels than those officially reported at that time.

59. A point made with both nuance and force in Christopher DeMuth, "Debt and Democracy," Legatum Institute, May 12, 2012. See http://www.hudson.org/files/publications/debt_and_democracy_lega tum.pdf.

60. The U.S. White House Office of Management and Budget, Historical Tables, Table 3.2: Outlays by Function and Subfunction: 1962–2017. See http://www.whitehouse.gov/omb/budget/Historicals. These definitions and estimates of national defense expenditure trends comes from the White House—the office of the commander in chief.

61. International Institute for Strategic Studies, The Military Balance 2012, March 2012, Figure: Comparative Defense Statistics. See http://www.iiss.org/ publications/military-balance/the-military-balance-2012/press-statement/figure-comparative-defence-statistics.

62. Dwight D. Eisenhower Presidential Library and Museum, Farewell Radio and Television Address to the American People, January 17, 1961. See http://www.eisenhower.archives.gov/all_about_ike/speeches/farewell_address.pdf.

63. $49.6 billion vs. $29.5 billion (in current dollars). Defense spending from the U.S. White House Office of Management and Budget, Historical Tables, Table 3.1: Outlays by Superfunction and Function, 1960–2017. See http://www.whitehouse.gov/omb/budget/Historicals; government transfers to individuals from Bureau of Economic Analysis, Personal Current Transfer Receipts. See http://www.bea.gov/iTable /iTableHtml.cfm?reqid=70&step=30&isuri=1&7028=-1&7040 =-1&7083=Levels&7031=0&7022=7&7023=0&7024=Non-In dustry&7025=0&7026=00000&7027=-1&7001=47&7029 =7&7090=70&7033=-1.

64. There had been exceptions to this generalization—pension payments for veterans exceeded defense budgets in the period after the Civil War, for instance—but they were just that: exceptions.

65. The comparison is admittedly imperfect. Current dollars are not adjusted for inflation, so they exaggerate the dimensions of the true increases in spending over time. As a matter of pure arithmetic, however, an inflation-adjusted contrast of trends in defense and entitlement spending would make the increases in entitlement spending look even more massive in relation to those in defense spending.

66. U.S. Department of Defense, Sustainable U.S. Global Leadership: Priorities for 21st-Century Defense, January 2012. See http://www.defense. gov/news/Defense_Strategic_Guidance.pdf.

67. Ibid., 3.

68. U.S. White House Office of Management and Budget, Historical Tables,

Table 3.1: Outlays by Superfunction and Function, 1960–2017. See http://www.whitehouse.gov/omb/budget/Historicals.

69. Sara Murray, "Nearly Half of U.S. Lives in Household Receiving Government Benefit," WSJ Economics Blog, *Wall Street Journal,* October 5, 2011. See http://blogs.wsj.com/economics/2011/10/05/nearly-half-of-households-receive-some-government-benefit/.

70. Felicia Sonmez, "RNC slams Obama 'You didn't build that' remark in conference call," *Washington Post,* July 23, 2012. See http://www.washingtonpost.com/blogs/election-2012/post/on-conference-call-with-business-owners-rnc-slams-obama-you-didnt-build-that-remark/2012/07/23/gJQAgACu4W_blog.html.

71. Nicholas Eberstadt, *The Poverty of the 'Poverty Rate': Measure and Mismeasure of Want in Modern America* (Washington, D.C.: American Enterprise Institute, 2008).

72. Cf., for example, Kip Hagopian and Lee Ohanian, "The Mismeasure of Inequality," *Policy Review,* no. 174 (August/September 2012). See http://www.hoover.org/publications/policy-review/article/123566. For a more technical analysis, see Orazio P. Attanasio, Erich Battistin, and Mario Padula, *Inequality in Living Standards since 1980: Income Tells Only a Small Part of the Story.* (Washington, D.C.: AEI Press, 2010).

73. The National Commission on Fiscal Responsibility of Reform, "The Moment of Truth," December 2010, p. 10. See http://www.fiscalcommission.gov/sites/fiscalcommission.gov/files/documents/TheMomentofTruth12_1_2010.pdf.

74. Alan J. Auerbach and William G. Gale, "Tempting Fate: The Federal Budget Outlook," June 30, 2011, p 16. See http://elsa.berkeley.edu/~auerbach/temptingfate.pdf.

75. Board of Governors of the Federal Reserve System, "Flow of Funds Account of the Unites States: Flows and Outstandings, First Quarter 2012," June 7, 2012. See http://www.federalreserve.gov/releases/z1/current/z1.pdf.

76. For an insightful assessment of this risk, see Barry Eichengreen, *Exorbitant Privilege: The Rise and Fall of the Dollar and the Future of the International Monetary System* (New York: Oxford University Press, 2011).

PART II

❧❧

Dissenting Points of View

Have We Become
a "Nation of Takers"?

≥≤

William A. Galston

NICHOLAS EBERSTADT assembles a host of empirical trends to prove a moral conclusion: the growth of the entitlement state over the past half-century has undermined the sturdy self-reliance that has long characterized most Americans, replacing it with a culture of dependence that not only distorts our government but also threatens the American experiment. This claim raises two large questions: Do these trends represent a full and fair account of what has taken place since 1960? And do they warrant the conclusion Eberstadt urges on his readers? After some brief reflections on the former question, I devote the bulk of my remarks to the latter.

WHAT HAS HAPPENED
IN THE PAST HALF-CENTURY?

As far as I can tell, Eberstadt's charts and statistics accurately represent the trends on which he focuses. But they are not the whole truth. In the first place, Eberstadt's accounting does not include all of the public policies that constitute entitlements as he defines them. Tax expenditures—special deductions and exemptions from, and credits against, otherwise taxable income—now constitute more than $1.1 trillion annually and they disproportionately benefit upper-income families. In an article published in the *Weekly Standard*, Andrew Hanson, Zackary Hawley, and Ike Brannon give an example:

Someone with a $1 million mortgage who earns over $300,000 a year could see the government essentially giving him a $20,000-a-year subsidy for his home, while a home-owner making $70,000 a year with a $150,000 mortgage would not receive a penny, since his puny deduction (under $2,000) would be less than the standard deduction.

But suppose we consider only the list of entitlement programs on which Eberstadt focuses. Based on his presentation, one might imagine that U.S. households have become far more dependent on public programs in recent decades. This seems not to be the case, however. A Congressional Budget Report (CBO) report released in October 2011 found that government transfers did not grow as a share of household market income between 1979 (a cyclical peak in the economy) and 2007 (another such peak) but rather oscillated between 10 and 12 percent. From the beginning to the end of that period, Social Security was unchanged at 6 percent of market income; health-care programs (primary Medicare, Medicaid, and the Children's Health Insurance Program) rose from under 2 percent to a bit less than 4 percent while all other transfer programs declined.

There was a change in the distribution of these transfers, however: the share going to the poorest households declined significantly. In 1979, households in the lowest income quintile received fully 54 percent of federal transfer payments, but by 2007 that figure had fallen to only 36 percent—a reduction of one-third. Put another way, during that period, households with low-wage or nonworking adults got less, while households in the middle and upper middle classes got more. If there is a problem of growing dependence, these figures suggest that it is located more in Middle America than in the ranks of the poor and near-poor. This possibility raises the question (to which I will return in the next section) of whether transfers going to families conducting themselves in accordance with middle-class norms of work and child-rearing represent dependence in any sense that gives rise to moral concern.

At least three other long-cycle trends need to be taken into account as well if we are to understand what is happening in our society and how we might respond. In the first place, we are an aging society. The massive investments in public schools and university expansion at the height of the baby boom have given way increasingly to the funding of hospitals and nursing homes. And while we typically regard the costs of dependence at the beginning of life as primarily the responsibility of families, this is much less true for dependence at the end of life. It is easy to see why. Aging brings expanding needs for complex and costly medical procedures that exceed the resources of average families. And no matter how hard they try, middle-aged adults often find that caring for aging parents in a family setting requires strength and skills they simply do not possess.

A second trend has exacerbated the consequences of aging: the near-disappearance of the pensions and health insurance for retirees that employers provided during the decades after the World War II. America's dominance of the global industrial economy gave employers the market power to set prices high enough to fund generous contracts with union-ized employees. As the devastated nations of Europe and Asia recovered and international competition intensified, the postwar bargain in the United States broke down, and gov-ernment stepped into the breach. For many Americans, Social Security became the primary (not supplemental) source of retirement income, and Medicare made up the difference between having and going without health insurance.

The third trend is macroeconomic. During the generation after World War II, the economy grew briskly, and the fruits of that growth were widely shared. Since then, growth has slowed, and the distribution of gains has become more con-centrated at the top. Between 1947 and 1973, incomes of families in the bottom quintile rose by 117 percent; in the middle quintile, by 103 percent; at the top, by 88 percent. From 1973 to 2000, in contrast, the bottom quintile rose by only 12 percent, the middle by 25 percent, and the top by 66 percent. And in the seven years of the twenty-first century before the Great Recession struck, family incomes at the bottom actually fell by 6 percent and stagnated for everyone else (except for those at the very top). Since 1973, meanwhile, costs for big-ticket items such as higher education and health care have risen far faster the family incomes, increasing pressure on the public sector to step into the breach.

So there are reasons—in my view, compelling ones—why the federal government has undertaken major new responsibilities during the past half-century. Even so, we still have a problem: a huge gap between the promises we have made and the resources we have been willing to devote to fulfilling them. One way or another, we must close this gap. But the moral heart of this fiscal challenge is not dependence but rather a dangerous combination of self-interest, myopia, and denial.

What Is "Dependence"?

To understand why I subordinate dependence to these other concerns, we must begin by clarifying the meaning of the term. One thing is clear at the outset: the dependence/independence dyad is too crude to capture the complexity of social relations. At a minimum, we must take account of a third term, "interdependence," and the norm of reciprocity that undergirds it. When I do something for you that you would be hard-pressed to do for yourself and you respond by helping me with something I find difficult, we depend on one another and are the stronger for it.

Well-functioning societies are replete with relations of this sort and use them as models for public policy. But the move from families and small groups to large-scale collective action makes a difference. Reciprocity becomes extended not only demographically and geographically but also chronologically. Political communities exist not just for the here and now but for future generations as well. Much contemporary public policy rests on temporally extended interdependence—in other terms, on an intergenerational compact. When we consent to deductions from our salary to help fund our parents' retirement, it is with the expectation that our children will do the same for us. This compact is practically sustainable and morally acceptable, but only with the proviso that the burdens we impose on our children are not disproportionate to the burdens we ourselves are willing to bear. The terms of interdependence matter, not just the fact of it. And so—to descend to cases—if we can honor promises to the current generation of working Americans only by imposing heavier sacrifices on the next generation, then something has gone awry. But—to repeat—"dependence" is the wrong characterization of the problem.

So is the concept of "entitlement." To be entitled to something is not necessarily to be dependent on it—at least not in a way that should trouble us. Consider the definition Eberstadt provides on page 4: "Government entitlement payments are benefits to which a person holds an established right under law (i.e., to which a person is entitled). A defining feature of these payments (also sometimes officially referred to as government transfers to individuals) is that they are 'benefits received for which no current service is performed.'"

Note that many nongovernmental relations have the same structure. If I use my life savings to purchase a retirement annuity, I have a legally enforceable expectation of receiving over time the stream of income specified in the contract. When I begin receiving these payments, I am performing no "current service" in exchange for them. And I certainly "depend" on these payments to fund my living expenses when I am no longer working. But surely I am not dependent in the way that so concerned Daniel Patrick Moynihan.

I do not see why transferring this case to the public sector makes a moral difference. Suppose someone pays into a government account throughout his working life, in effect purchasing an annuity to fund his retirement. If the income stream is actuarially fair, then he can expect to get back the equivalent of what he contributed. He may do better or worse, of course. If he lives until ninety-five, he will get back more; if he dies at seventy, less. Relying on these payments doesn't make him dependent in any morally troubling sense.

Social Security works this way for millions of Americans. For many others, it is more complicated: some can expect to receive more than the actuarial value of their contributions, others less. Americans in the latter category are helping to fund retirement for those in the former. In effect, some workers are relying on others for a portion of their retirement income. But again, this quantitative premise does not imply a disturbing moral conclusion. When Moynihan worried about dependence, he was not thinking about individuals who have worked hard all their lives in low-wage jobs but whose payroll taxes do not suffice to fund what society regards as a dignified retirement.

I would make a similar argument about the Earned Income Tax Credit, which supplements the earnings of low-wage workers. Since the Gerald Ford administration, the political parties have usually agreed on the proposition that people who work full-time, year-round shouldn't live in poverty, and neither should their families. To the extent that market wages do not suffice to meet this standard, the public sector should step in to fill the gap. While these low-wage workers are not self-sufficient, they are not dependent either, because dependency is a matter of character, not arithmetic.

In a similar vein, Ron Haskins, one of the architects of the 1996 welfare reform, points out that public expenditures under the reforms were often higher than for the Aid to Families with Dependent Children (AFDC) program they replaced. The difference: These new outlays were designed to promote work on the part of welfare recipients who had previously received monthly checks without meaningful work requirements. The government subsidized transportation, child care, and health care, but only if recipients of these benefits entered the paid workforce within a reasonable period. In one sense, these individuals were even more dependent on the public purse than they had been in the old system. In another sense, however, they were becoming less dependent, because they were assuming more responsibility to provide for themselves and their families.

We are in no way troubled when children depend on their parents—that's the way it's supposed to be. While we sympathize with the elderly who depend on caregivers for assistance, we are not morally troubled by that either. And it is acceptable for society to help those adults who are doing their best to provide for themselves but cannot manage to do so. Our concern focuses on those who could be doing more to help themselves but choose not to do so. That is the kind of dependence that troubles us. To the extent that specific public programs exacerbate it, we have good reason to alter them, as we did in 1996. It is far from clear that programs like Social Security and Medicare create that type of dependence whatsoever. But what about means-tested programs such as Medicaid, eligibility for which depends on status (such as poverty) rather than activity (such as work)? Do they increase dependence? Again, consider the low-wage worker in a job that does not provide health insurance. Given current costs on the individual market, that worker is in no position to purchase insurance for himself. So his choices reduce to three: he can go without needed health care, he can seek charity care delivered through the voluntary sector, or he can participate in public programs financed mostly by higher-income taxpayers. I suppose someone could argue that receiving charitable care (if it is available) produces less dependency than partici-pating in Medicaid. (I'll confess that I don't see why.) But the broader point is that if the individual is doing the best he can to provide for himself but falls short, helping him out with life's essentials does not contribute to dependence.

Indeed, one could argue that it does just the reverse. When society commits itself to the principle that a serious and sus-tained effort to provide for oneself and one's family should be rewarded, independence becomes more rather than less likely. There is no necessary relation between the growth of means-tested government benefits and the increase in the kind of dependence we care about from a moral point of view.

There is a moral hazard, however. At some point the desire to ease the plight of the poor who are doing the best they can shades over into assistance for the not-so-poor whose lives would be harder but not unworkable without it. In the past five years, for example, the number of individuals par-ticipating in the Supplemental Nutrition Assistance Program (SNAP, formerly known as food stamps) has exploded from 26 million to 46 million, and annual costs have risen from $33 billion to more than $75 billion. Much of this stems from the Great Recession, which swelled the ranks of the unemployed, especially those out of work for more than six months. But some of it is attributable to the liberalization of eligibility standards and expansion of benefits during the past decade. It is plausible (though hardly certain) that these changes may have encouraged dependency among some percentage of the beneficiaries—especially those who were not living in poverty prior to receiving benefits. But there is no moral algorithm that tells us whether it is better for public programs to help too many people or too few.

Complicating Eberstadt's argument are two other concerns that we must distinguish from dependence per se. First is the balance of activities that government conducts. For example, Social Security is not just an ensemble of individual relationships between workers and the government, but also a massive program that pays out hundreds of billions of dollars each year to 56 million recipients—more than 15 percent of the entire population. During the past half century, as Eberstadt rightly suggests, Social Security and programs like it have transformed the federal government's balance sheet. Much of the federal budget now consists of dedicated revenues from entitlement programs and (on the other side of the balance sheet) payments to those program's beneficiaries. In so doing, the government is neither providing nor consuming resources and services. It is transferring purchasing power to certain groups of individuals, often with considerable efficiency. (By private-sector standards, the Social Security Administration is a well-run organization.)

While these transfers swell the government's revenues and outlays, they do less to alter the overall allocation of resources than do equivalent levels of taxing and spending for an all-out military mobilization—that is, if revenues and outlays attributable to these transfers are in balance over time.

But as we know, they are not, which brings us to the heart of the matter. The growth of the entitlement state is coming at the expense of the public investments—such as infrastructure and research—that spur economic growth and social progress, and they are now threatening to squeeze national defense as well.

The moral issue here is not dependence; it is myopia or (more bluntly) generational selfishness. If we do not change course, we risk leaving to our children and grandchildren a less prosperous and advanced society and a less promising future. One way or another, we have to restrain consumption in favor of investment—by increasing revenues for investment, decreasing outlays for entitlements, or (most likely) some of both.

Eberstadt observes that the heart of the problem lies in the overlapping spheres of retirement and health care. But here again, some distinctions are needed. Social Security has grown and will continue to grow at a modest pace. Restoring the program to long-term solvency requires some well-understood choices and represents a relatively tractable problem. Health care is very different; it consumes an ever-increasing share of our GDP, and its growth reflects the complex interplay of technological advances, expanding individual aspirations, and changing social norms. We cannot easily decouple programs such as Medicare and Medicaid from the provision of health care as a whole.

The moral questions at issue go far deeper than either

dependence or myopia. Since the seventeenth century, philosophers have advocated expanding scientific knowledge to relieve pain and suffering, extend human life, and perhaps even abolish death. Not until relatively recently did research-based medical advances bring these aspirations within reach. Open-heart surgery, organ transplants, joint replacements—these and many other innovations help millions of people lead functional lives far longer than their parents could have done. But even when performed efficiently, these procedures require state-of-the art technology and highly trained practitioners. They are inherently expensive, and because of the human goods at stake, it is hard to argue that income should determine whether individuals have access to them.

Still, we have no choice but to confront the aggregate costs of our commitment to equality. The Affordable Care Act has triggered an overdue national discussion, which will continue (I suspect for at least a decade) until we have found a socially acceptable formula for bringing our hopes and our resources into a more sustainable balance. I doubt that moral considerations such as dependence will be of much help in resolving this issue.

REAL PROBLEMS OF DEPENDENCE

Eberstadt presents no direct evidence that the growth of the federal government has changed Americans' character or weakened their moral fiber, perhaps because it is very hard to find. Indeed, in-depth examinations of public attitudes suggest the reverse. In 2009, for example, the Pew Social Mobility Project asked a representative sample of Americans what is essential or very important to getting ahead. Ninety-two percent said hard work; 89 percent, ambition; 83 percent, a good education. In contrast, factors such as race (15 percent), gender (16 percent), luck (21 percent), and family wealth (28 percent) ranked at the bottom. Asked about the role of government in fostering economic mobility, 36 percent of respondents thought it did more to help than to hurt, but many more—46 percent—endorsed the opposite view. A follow-up survey two years later revealed that the share of Americans who considered government helpful for mobility had declined to only 27 percent, while those who thought it detrimental had risen to 52 percent.

That is not to say that government has no role. Large majorities thought that public policy could do more to increase jobs in the United States and reduce college and health-care costs. But in their view, mobility-enhancing programs help individuals help themselves. If the growth of government has created a culture of dependence, it is hard to discern the evidence in these surveys, which are representative of a large body of research.

Eberstadt does offer some indirect evidence of cultural change, two instances of which warrant sustained attention. There is little doubt that the Social Security Disability Insurance program (SSDI) is subject to serious abuse. During the past decade, the number of workers receiving monthly benefits has soared from 5.3 million to 8.6 million. And because SSDI recipients qualify for Medicare after receiving benefits for two years, few working-age beneficiaries leave the program once they have entered. By 2010, annual benefits had reached $115 billion, plus $75 billion in added Medicare costs.

The variation in acceptance rates across states and across time suggests that generous interpretations of partly subjective criteria can result in the admission of applicants who could work part-time or even full-time. In Puerto Rico the approval rate rose from 36 percent in 2006 to 69 percent in 2011. One judge in San Juan reportedly approved 98 percent of the cases brought to him.

Exacerbating these problems, the program's inflexible design encourages all-or-nothing approaches. According to economists David Autor and Mark Duggan, "The program provides strong incentives to applicants and beneficiaries to remain permanently out of the labor force, and it provides no incentive to employers to implement cost-effective accommodations that enable employees with work limitations to remain on the job."[1] After examining Social Security data, two other economists, Nicole Maestas and Kathleen Mullen, estimate that close to one-fifth of current recipients could work and earn enough to exceed the threshold at which they no longer would qualify for benefits. It is plausible that if the kinds of accommodations Autor and Duggan favor were implemented, the number who could work at least part-time would be even higher.

The implications of these problems are less clear than are the problems themselves. When people are given a choice between working with physical pain or emotional distress and not working, some will choose to receive benefits rather than toughing it out. If the program did not exist, they would not have this choice. In that sense, the program encourages financial dependence.

But this is not necessarily evidence of a deep cultural change. The desire to get something for nothing is a hardy perennial of human nature, not a late-twentieth-century invention. U.S. history is replete with swindles and get-rich-quick schemes. What may have changed is the willingness of taxpayers to fund programs that prefer compassion to tough love. Over the past three decades, efforts to tighten up the program have repeatedly wrecked on the shoals of public resistance. Tales of individual suffering move many voters, and a prosperous society has been willing to fund public compassion—so far. It will be interesting to see what happens when these generous instincts run up against inevitable future efforts to rein in massive budget deficits.

Far more disturbing than the abuses of a single program is the evidence Eberstadt presents of the long-term withdrawal of working-age men from the labor force. Fifty years ago, more than 85 percent of men age twenty and over were in the labor force. Ever before the Great Recession hit, that figure had declined by ten percentage points, and it has dropped more in the ensuing years. During the same period, female labor force participation rose by more than twenty points, stabilizing at around 60 percent in the late 1990s.

Why have so many men checked out? Eberstadt is sure that the "entitlement society" is responsible; without all the programs that enable men to get by without working, the flight from employment "could not have been possible." Perhaps so. Still, although men and women are equally eligible to participate in these programs, they seem to have responded quite differently, at least in the aggregate. For example, nearly as many women (4.1 million) as men (4.5 million) receive disability benefits, but that has not kept the ranks of women in the paid workforce from swelling.

Labor economists do not agree with Eberstadt's causal argument. For example, they point out that in recent decades, women have been far more willing than men to take advantage of expanding educational opportunities, and the enhanced labor market options that come with them. Prior to the cohort of children born in the mid-1950s, the percentage of men with four-year college degrees exceeded that of women. In every year since then, the percentage of women with bachelor's degrees has exceeded that of men. This disparity can be traced, in part, to a widening gap between male and female high school graduation rates. For cohorts born up to the late 1940s, there was no difference. Since then, every year, higher percentages of women have graduated from high school. The doors of public schools are open equally to boys and girls, and there is no discrimination against men in college admissions or federal student loans. No evidence exists that men gain less than women from higher levels of education. The growth of the entitlement state cannot be responsible for gender-based educational disparities—at least not directly.

One key trend is the falling earnings of men who have less than a college education. Since 1979, while real wages have risen for women at every educational level, they have risen only for men with bachelor's degrees or higher. Over the past three decades, after taking inflation into account, less educated men have experienced income losses of between 5 and 25 percent.

Operating in tandem with globalization and deunionization, technological change has wiped out many of the jobs that offered middle-class incomes to workers with limited educational attainment. But while most women have moved into higher-skilled occupations, most men have moved into lower-paying service jobs—if they have remained in the labor force at all. Many have not, and labor economists think that the decline in real earnings offers one reason.

There is evidence to support two other possible explanations for falling male labor participation. The mid-twentieth century industrial economy put a premium on the kinds of attributes that men tended to possess, but the reverse seems to be the case in today's economy. As David Autor puts it, recent research suggests that "women disproportionately possess the combination of cognitive and interpersonal skills that are valuable in information and technology-rich work environments where the importance of physically demanding and repetitive tasks has been greatly diminished." Simply put, there is less demand for what men bring to the table and more for what women do.

Finally, there is evidence that changes in family structures during the past two generations have had worse consequences for adolescent and young adult males than for their female counterparts. Although the divorce rate is down from its peak in the early 1980s, more children experience marital breakups than was the case in the 1960s. In addition, the percentage of children born out of wedlock to parents who never marry has soared. As a result, fewer children now reach age eighteen living with both biological parents, and those who do not live with their two biological parents spend most of their time in households headed by their mother rather than their father. While this situation is not good for girls, it is much worse for boys, who are more likely to develop disciplinary problems and, as we have seen, to drop out before receiving their high school diplomas. These young men face dismal prospects in today's labor market.

Some have argued that the growth of the entitlement state is principally responsible for the changes in family structure working to the disadvantage of young men. Perhaps this is true to some extent. But in any event, it is hardly the main story. As recently as the 1960s, many women married and stayed married for economic reasons. But as their prospects brightened in the paid workforce, they became less dependent on men for income and security. The divorce revolution of the 1970s accelerated this trend, as many young women came to believe that it was safer to rely on their own earning power than on the fidelity of prospective mates. As the educational attainment and earnings of men fell relative to that of women (and in many cases in absolute terms as well), women became less likely to regard available males as "marriageable." Women who had seized opportunities to better themselves were reluctant to tie themselves to men who might well drag them back down. We are dealing, in short, with a complex interplay of economic and social change that cannot be traced, or reduced, to shifts in public policy.

CONCLUSION

By bringing together and concisely presenting a wealth of data, Eberstadt has performed a real service. He dramatizes the remarkable rise of the entitlement state and issues warnings about its consequences that we must consider seriously. Still, there are good reasons to question the causal link between entitlement programs and dependence—at least the kind of dependence that should concern us. To be sure, Americans want a reasonable level of security in their retirement years, and they think that government programs such as Social Security and Medicare are essential to that security. But they continue to believe that government is no substitute for hard work, ambition, and the perseverance that enables young people to complete their education and put it to work in the job market. They think that government should make reasonable provision for the poor and disabled, but they do not believe that government should enable people who could be independent to depend on the efforts of others. To the extent that current programs turn out to be inconsistent with that view, they will eventually be trimmed or abolished, as was AFDC in 1996.

Left unchecked, the programs we have created in the past half-century will make it difficult to stabilize our finances, to invest in the future, and to defend the nation. These are compelling reasons to rethink the entitlement state. But they have little to do with an alleged culture of dependence, the evidence for which is thin at best. As long as we do our part, there is no harm in benefitting from programs we help sustain. As long as we contribute our share, taking is morally unproblematic. We can be a nation of takers, as long as we are a nation of givers as well. As long as we honor the norm of reciprocity for our compatriots and for posterity, we can steer a steady course.

Note

1. David H. Autor and Mark Duggan, "Supporting Work: A Proposal for Modernizing the U.S. Disability Insurance System," Center for American Progress and The Hamilton Project, December 2010, http://www.hamiltonproject.org/files/downloads_and_links/FINAL_Autor-DugganPaper.pdf

Civil Society
and the Entitlement State

— ≥≤ —

Yuval Levin

WITH HIS USUAL clear-eyed focus on the facts and his knack for seeing the most piquant details in a complex statistical picture, Nicholas Eberstadt offers a bracing history of the past few decades of American life, and a stern warning of even greater trouble to come.

The trouble is coming on two related fronts above all: a transformation of the sort of government we have, and a transformation of the sorts of citizens we are. It is only when we see these two in combination—as a grave threat to the character of American self-government—that we can fully appreciate the dangers inherent in the ballooning of the liberal welfare state. Eberstadt approaches that description of the problem, but does not quite take it up. It requires some additional reflection on the implications of the data he provides for America's political and civic institutions. And although that reflection might lead us to conclude that our problems run even deeper than Eberstadt suggests, it should also help us to see that solutions are possible if we set out to reform our governing institutions with a particular set of attitudes and aims—and perhaps that our becoming "takers" is not quite the right way to think of the problem we face.

Our reflection must begin with a general idea of the structure of American civic life, and the place of the government in it. This is a subject that has been peculiarly prominent in this intense election year. To a degree rarely seen in modern times, the 2012 presidential election appears to be raising to the surface a set of starkly different visions about the relationship between the government and the citizen in American life.

These differences have mostly been made explicit by the political left, in an effort to articulate liberals' understanding of the character of the conservative reaction to the Obama years. In the conservative resistance to expansions of the reach and role of the federal government, and in the alternative fiscal plans drawn up by congressional Republicans since the 2010 elections, liberals believe they have seen the face of radical individualism and a complete rejection of all common endeavors and community undertakings. President Obama gave voice to this view in his comments in Roanoke, Virginia, on July 13, 2012, where he accused his opponents of a fanatical idolatry of individual achievement that willfully ignores the preconditions for success made possible by the larger society—which he identified more or less exclusively with the government. Numerous speakers at the 2012 Democratic National Convention made the same case, arguing, for instance, that (in the words of the convention's opening video) "government is the one thing we all belong to," and that (in the words of Rep. Barney Frank) "there are things that a civilized society needs that we can only do when we do them together, and when we do them together that's called government.[1]"

Conservatives have responded to these critics mostly by defending individual initiative and achievement, and so in effect confirming the Democrats' charges to some degree. A fuller response would have to marvel at the thin view of American life revealed in the left's critique of the right: a view that sees in our society only individuals and the government, and that neither discerns nor wants much of consequences in the space between the two.

But most of life is lived somewhere between those two, and American life in particular has given rise to unprecedented human flourishing because we have allowed the institutions that occupy the middle ground—the family, civil society, and the private economy—to thrive in relative freedom. Indeed, while the progressive view of government has long involved (and has been revealed once more in recent years to involve) the effort to shrink and clear the space between the individual and the state, the conservative view of government has long seen the purpose of the state as the creation, protection, and reinforcement of just that space. Most of what we do together is not done through government but through the institutions that exist between the individual and the state, and government exists to sustain the space in which those institutions, and with them our society, may thrive.

This means that government is crucially important, but it also means that limits on government are crucially import- ant—and for the very same reason. Without those limits, the state can gravely threaten the space for private life that it is charged with protecting. It can do so in two ways in partic- ular: by invading that space and attempting to fill it; and by collapsing that space under the weight of the government's sheer size, scope, and cost. In our time (and by that I mean the past several decades, not the past four years), both dan- gers have grown grave and alarming, and the space between the individual and the state—the space in which American life has always been lived—seems now to be in mortal peril.

On the one hand, we see a seemingly unending succession of government efforts to fill, rather than to guard, the space in which society thrives. In the past few years, for instance, we have seen unprecedented attacks on the freedom of religious institutions to operate in civil society if they are committed to moral views different from those of the people in power. But for far longer than that we have witnessed the growth of government efforts to stand in for the institutions of civil society, to treat players in the private economy as agents of government policy, and at times even to substitute for the family in a variety of ways.

And on the other hand, we have seen the sheer girth of the growing welfare state begin to cast a giant shadow over our society—as our growing indebtedness claims an increasing share of the next generation's material wealth for the sake of providing benefits to satisfy the current generation's material wants. The space in which our society lives threatens to collapse under the weight of that debt even as it is increasingly invaded by the very welfare state we are funding with all that borrowing.

And here we come again to Eberstadt's two kinds of warnings about the ballooning of the welfare state: one warning about how the trends he describes are changing our government, and another warning about how those trends are changing our citizens. The two are deeply connected in some less than obvious ways. It is true—as Eberstadt suggests—that the very extension of the reach of government benefits must have some effect on the character of our self-governing citizenry. It is a stunning fact that, as he shows, a majority of American households now receive some government benefit, and there can be no doubt that this fact has an effect on how we understand what it means to be a citizen. Because not only the poor but the great mass of citizens become recipients of benefits, people in the middle class come to approach their government as claimants, not as self-governing citizens, and to approach the social safety net not as a great majority of givers eager to make sure that a small minority of recipients are spared from devastating poverty but as a mass of dependents demanding what they are owed. It is hard to imagine an ethic better suited to undermine the moral basis of a free society.

But there is a more to the problem, because the source of any counterforce to this tendency to corrupt the ethic of self-government must come from our institutions of civic culture and civil society, and as we have seen the precious space in which those institutions exist is itself under threat. In a free society, the government does not take the lead in shaping the citizens. Self-governing citizens are mostly shaped in that space between the individual and the state—that space where family, civil society, religion, culture, and the economy form our dispositions and proclivities. And the simultaneous invasion of that space by government and imposition on that space by government makes it very difficult for those forming institutions to function. Liberal democracy has always depended upon a kind of person it does not produce, and which must be formed by institutions that are not themselves liberal or political, but that are given room to function within our liberal society. The growth of our welfare state increasingly puts those fonts of the republican virtues in peril.

In essence, our country is increasingly exhausting itself just to fund the means of its own further exhaustion. It is not quite dependence that is the problem here, as Eberstadt seems at times to suggest. It is rather that we are draining away our civic energies by the sheer effort required to sustain the liberal welfare state even as—through the growth of that welfare state—we are undercutting the means by which we might replenish those energies.

This exhaustion is not merely a function of the size of our entitlement and benefit regime, but also of its immense inefficiency. That inefficiency means that the level of benefits we receive from the government does not grow in proportion to the level of resources we devote to it—we spend more and more for less and less, and it is in the spending as much as in the taking that we run the risk of undermining the ethic of our democratic republic.

The largest single portion of our welfare state—that which provides health-care benefits—helps to illustrate this point. As Eberstadt points out, two-thirds of income-based benefits and transfers over the past five decades have flowed through one program: Medicaid. And the growth of our broader benefit regime over the past few decades, as well as its projected growth over the next few, is attributable to an extraordinary and underappreciated extent to increasing spending on health benefits, through both Medicaid for the poor and (especially) Medicare for the elderly.

The federal government got into the business of paying for health insurance in 1965. In 1971, by which time Medicare and Medicaid had reached their mature and fully functional forms, spending on those two programs combined accounted for 1 percent of our gross domestic product, according to the Congressional Budget Office (CBO). That figure then doubled and doubled again, so that 40 years later, by 2011, federal health spending accounted for 5.6 percent of the GDP. This astounding rate of growth has dwarfed the growth of everything else our government spends money on—including other benefits to individuals. Indeed, conservatives who complain about the general growth of government spending rarely consider just how thoroughly the growth of health-care spending has defined the larger trend. The figure for all *non*-health care federal spending combined (including Social Security, defense, all other benefit programs, everything but interest on the debt) was 17.1 percent of GDP in 1971 and was again 17.1 percent of GDP in 2011, according to CBO, while health spending more than quintupled over that period. In essence, the net growth in government as a percentage of the economy in these four decades has been entirely a function of federal health spending.

And without major reforms of these programs, that growth will only continue. By 2020, CBO projects Medicare and Medicaid (together with the new entitlements created by the new health care law) will account for 6.9 percent of GDP. In 2030 it will be 9.2 percent. In 2040, CBO projects it will be 11.4 percent of GDP, and by 2050 it will be almost 14 percent. And all other spending combined is projected by CBO to actually *decline* some as a percentage of the economy over this period. On the course we are on, in other words, the federal government will become a health-insurance provider with some unusual side ventures, like an army and a navy.

And yet, this ballooning of health spending may not have quite the effect on its beneficiaries that Eberstadt ascribes to our growing welfare state, because although it involves more and more public dollars, it does not actually involve more and more generous benefits and coverage. Spending is growing because health-care costs are out of control (and those costs, in turn, are out of control in large part because of the open-ended nature of federal health care commitments). That means that our health entitlement programs are spending more and more for the same thing. It looks like more and more to the government, but not to the recipients of benefits.

Today's Medicare recipients are probably not much more dependent on the program than were Medicare beneficiaries in 1980, even though the program costs more than four times what it did then in inflation-adjusted dollars. Medicare is a little more generous (mostly because it now includes a prescription-drug benefit), but a greater proportion of doctors now refuse to accept Medicare patients, as the program's payment rates continue to dip. Today's Medicaid beneficiaries are not much more dependent on the program than they would have been in 1980 either, even though it again costs the federal government more than four times what it did then, in inflation-adjusted dollars. It's certainly true that more Americans receive Medicaid benefits, but the growth in beneficiaries is not nearly on par with the growth in spending, and the benefits they receive are really not more generous in any meaningful way than they would have been several decades ago. Indeed, for Medicaid patients, access to doctors is far more limited that it used to be, again because Medicaid underpays physicians even as it bankrupts the states and the federal government.

So why are we spending more and more for the same thing? A key reason is the immense inefficiency of our entitlement system—a point Eberstadt does not take up much. Medicare, Medicaid, and the tax exclusion for employer-provided insurance (a middle-class subsidy almost as large as Medicare and Medicaid) are the primary causes of that inefficiency, but our system of means-tested assistance to the poor would also have to be judged dreadfully ineffective in relation to its growing cost. We spend 300 percent more on per-capita means tested benefits today than we did in the 1970s, but the poverty level has not changed much at all.

This inefficiency is directly connected to a further profound problem: the growth of cynicism toward our welfare state. In our everyday experience, the bureaucratic state presents itself not as a benevolent provider of benefits and protector of the needy but as a slow, fat, feckless, and unresponsive behemoth. Largely free of competition, most administrative agencies do not have to answer directly to public preferences, and so have developed in ways that make their own operations easier (or their own employees more contented) but that grow increasingly distant from the way we live in an age of endless variety and choice.

Unresponsive ineptitude is not merely an annoyance. The sluggishness of the welfare state drains it of its moral force. The crushing weight of bureaucracy permits neither efficiency nor idealism. It thus robs us of a good part of the energy of democratic capitalism and encourages a corrosive cynicism that cannot help but undermine the very moral vision that has shaped the liberal welfare state.

All of this adds up not merely, or even mostly, to a nation of takers. It leaves us, rather, a nation at risk of becoming incapable of rising to the challenge of self-government. It is often said now that our political system is paralyzed by division. But that is a misdiagnosis. In the past decade, we have seen the enactment of, among other things, a large tax reform (the Bush tax cuts), a large education reform, a huge reorganization of our domestic security agencies, a reform of corporate governance (Sarbanes-Oxley), a new Medicare benefit, a massive response to the financial crisis (including several stimulus bills, an unprecedented bank rescue, a bailout of auto companies, and more, crossing two administrations of different parties), a huge health-care reform, a huge financial-regulation reform, and a budget deal with 10-year sequestration spending caps. That is a very active period of major federal legislation—certainly more active than the prior decade or the one before that. There is just one thing we cannot do: We cannot address the fiscal crisis being brought upon us by the welfare state. And that is less a function of division than of agreement—we do not really want to address that crisis. We want to keep the benefits flowing, but we don't want to pay the price. So benefits continue to grow and our debt continues to mount.

The failure to address this problem is the most glaring failure of responsible self-government in our time. It is in part a function of our desire to pretend there is no problem and to ignore the sorry shape and dire consequences of the liberal welfare state. But it has also been a function of a poverty of policy imagination, born of a failure to understand the nature of the problem we confront.

Because the danger of our ballooning welfare state is fundamentally a danger to that essential space between the individual and the state, the solution to our problems will need to come through a re-opening of that space, and through a rethinking of the role of government that assigns to it again the task of securing that space. The reforms we require need not be directed first and foremost to reducing benefits as such but rather to restraining the reach of government and to controlling the growth of its costs.

Is there a way to provide the kinds of benefits we have come to want our government to provide—income and health benefits for the old and for the poor—without the kind of ballooning of government's size and role that we have experienced? I believe there is, if we understand the purpose of such benefits as enabling access to the private economy (rather than shielding beneficiaries from it), and if we allow the means by which such benefits are provided to be shaped by modern markets rather than by the old social-democratic ideal of the provider state.

When it comes to providing services rather than cash—especially in health care, which is the core of our welfare state—the government should use its resources to create markets and enable competition, rather than to replace markets and command supply and demand. And when it comes to providing direct cash benefits to the poor, we should seek to follow the model of the welfare reforms of the 1990s—a defined federal role supporting state efforts that are linked to work requirements and strictly means tested. The government should not seek to stand in for the private economy, civil society, and the family but rather to strengthen them and to enable the poor and the vulnerable to access that space between the individual and the state where human thriving really happens.

Such reforms—again, especially the health-benefit reforms —would dramatically reduce the cost of our government. But, more importantly, they would move beyond the liberal model of the welfare state toward an approach that seeks to refortify and to revive the space between the citizen and the state, rather than to collapse or to invade that space. They would respond to the crisis of the welfare state with a vision of American life beyond the welfare state—a vision informed by the ideals that formed our republic but that responds in practical ways to the needs and desires of our 21st century nation. They would help us become once again a nation of self-governing citizens, and to avoid the sorry fate that Nicholas Eberstadt's grim but timely warning has laid before us.

Note

1. Rep. Barney Frank (D-Mass), addressing the 2012 Democratic Convention on Thursday, September 6. See http://www.c-spanvideo.org/ program/ConventionDayTh.

EPILOGUE:
Response to Levin and Galston

≳≲

NICHOLAS EBERSTADT

I DEEPLY APPRECIATE THESE incisive and thoughtful reflections by Yuval Levin and William Galston—friends and colleagues. Both of these challenge us to think deeper and harder about America's entitlement dilemma: but Dr. Levin and Professor Galston proceed along very different paths. Let me therefore address each briefly, and in turn.

Bill Galston offers a careful and powerful critique of my study, offering an alternative interpretation of some of the big trends that we both agree have transformed life in post-war America. He takes strong exception to the notion that we have become "a nation of takers," and emphasizes the important element of reciprocity in our social policies (as in our social relations)—elements he quite rightly wishes to strengthen in America, both today and tomorrow.

I am impressed by the cogency of his main arguments, but I am not ultimately persuaded by them. Although Professor Galston is incontestably correct when he states that the trends in entitlement program participation do not trace a totally smooth upward trajectory, and are indeed strongly influenced by particular social and macroeconomic changes over the past several generations, the plain fact is that entitlement programs have absorbed a larger and larger share of our national resources with every passing decade—and have enrolled a larger and larger share of our population as recipients every decade as well.

It is important to note that the rise in the prevalence of entitlement recipience has been driven mainly by a dramatic increase in the proportion of homes that accept "means-tested" benefits, supposedly poverty-related: as of 2009, over 100 million Americans were in households that sought and obtained such transfers. As of 2010, over 34 percent of American households were obtaining means-tested benefits—and nearly half of our nation's children lived in such households, according to Census Bureau data. Such basic facts, I believe, manifestly speak to a sea-change in American attitudes about what was once called "relief," more recently known as "welfare."

Reciprocity, as William Galston so compellingly emphasizes, is the foundation for any healthy and functional social relationship. My problem with our entitlement archipelago is precisely the lack of reciprocity. In theory, Social Security and Medicare are social insurance programs—and insurance arrangements are meant to embody the principles of reciprocity and solidarity. But neither Social Security nor Medicare is actuarially sound today—in fact, they never have been actuarially sound. They can only survive over the long term by taking resources from outsiders who have not participated in their programs. This is not reciprocity—nor is the gaming of the Disability Insurance trust fund (a moral hazard Galston highlights), nor the increasing predilection by ever less impoverished Americans to apply for "means-tested" benefits. To the contrary—all of this smacks of the something-for-nothing mentality that I see as all to integral to the rise of our modern entitlement state. I will be delighted if William Galston and likeminded citizens can restore more reciprocity to our public social programs: but I suspect this will not be possible without a decidedly smaller welfare state, with less influence in everyday American life, or without decidedly more self-reliance for Americans of every walk of life.

Where Professor Galston would hold that I am too alarmist about the state of our entitlement society, Dr. Levin suggests I am not nearly as alarmed as I should be. In his subtle, learned and highly informed contribution he makes the case that our entitlements pathology today is symptomatic of an even greater malaise: an abdication of the duties of self-governance that lie at the heart of successful constitutional democracy. He suggests that the objectives theoretically served by existing entitlement arrangements could in practice be accomplished, perhaps even more effectively, by a radical overhaul of our transfer programs and wholesale shift toward more market-oriented models of service provision. (We may note in passing that market transactions, unlike public resource transfers, always require a measure of reciprocity.)

I cannot contest Dr. Levin's deeper misgivings about the implications of our apparently metastasizing entitlement cancer for the greater health of our body politic. I share those concerns (though I very much doubt I could have put my finger on the philosophical and metaphysical dangers these pose to our very democratic system as beautifully as he just did). For their part, the general direction in which Dr. Levin would prefer to see entitlement reform progress sounds to be both commonsensical and ethically grounded. As he clearly realizes, however, such a transformation is much easier to envision than to actualize. Effecting such a transformation, I suspect, will not be possible without a prolonged, pitched, and bitter political struggle within our country. Such a transformation, further, will almost surely require a modern-day *Kulturkampf*: more often than not, these are not pretty to behold, and not pleasant to live through. I myself wonder whether we as a nation could move ourselves to overhaul our entitlement systems fundamentally, absent an existential crisis in which we have no other alternatives. I pray that the answer to this question is: yes. But I fear we may live to find out.

Together, Yuval Levin and William Galston have provided a splendid start to the conversation about our national entitlements problem. I can only hope that this conversation is joined by many other voices—and that the discussion will continue be informed by the same principled clarity and intelligent concern with which it has commenced.

About the Contributors

NICHOLAS EBERSTADT, a political economist and a demographer by training, holds the Henry Wendt Chair in Political Economy at American Enterprise Institute. He is also a senior adviser to the National Board of Asian Research, a member of Commission on Key National Indicators, and a member of the Global Agenda Council at the World Economic Forum. He researches and writes extensively on economic development, foreign aid, global health, demographics, and poverty. In 2012 he was awarded the Bradley Prize.

WILLIAM A. GALSTON is a political theorist. He holds the Zilkha Chair in Governance at the Brookings Institution. In addition he is College Park Professor at the University of Maryland. He was a senior adviser to President Bill Clinton on domestic policy.

YUVAL LEVIN is the Hertog Fellow at the Ethics and Public Policy Center, founding editor of *National Affairs* magazine, and a senior editor of EPPC's journal *The New Atlantis*. His areas of specialty include health care, entitlement reform, economic and domestic policy, science and technology policy, political philosophy, and bioethics. Mr. Levin served on the White House domestic policy staff under President George W. Bush, focusing on health care as well as bioethics and culture-of-life issues. Mr. Levin previously served as Executive Director of the President's Council on Bioethics, and as a congressional staffer.